Colonial America

cooperative learning activities*

by Susan Schneck and Mary Strohl

*Lessons easily adaptable to traditional classroom or work station settings

SCHOLASTIC
PROFESSIONAL **B**OOKS

New York • Toronto • London • Auckland • Sydney

About the Authors

Susan Schneck and Mary Strohl have many years combined experience in education and publishing. In 1986 they started their own studio, *Flights of Fancy*, specializing in children's activity products and elementary teaching materials. This is their second title for Scholastic Professional Books.

special thanks to

Patricia Scaffidi for sharing her experiences,
resources and insights into cooperative learning

and to

Mr. Isacco A. Valli, Assistant Director/Curator
Manitowoc Maritime Museum, Manitowoc, Wisconsin

CURR
E
162
.S36
1991

ISBN 0-590-49133-4

12 11 10 9 8 7

678/9

Printed in the U.S.A.

Table of Contents

Caleb
b. 1682

Abigail
b. 1686

Miles
b. 1690

Constance
b. 1694

Jacob
b. 1694

Humility

Joseph

The Cavendish Family in America

About This Book

Colonial America covers the growth of the thirteen separate colonies from 1690 to 1715, long after the pilgrims had settled in Massachusetts. Most colonies are fairly well established with working farms and a few small settlements and towns. In the first chapter we are introduced to the Cavendish family as they are preparing to leave England for the New World. We follow them through the first years of their settling in rural Pennsylvania. The family grows; their farm prospers. Caleb becomes a joiner in Philadelphia. Miles becomes a sailor, traveling to the other colonies and writing back to his family about what he sees.

Getting Started

1492		1620	1690	1715

To begin your studies, draw this time line on the board. Ask children to tell you the significance of the first two dates. (1492: Columbus discovered America. 1620: The Pilgrims came to Massachusetts.) Tell the children that they are going to study Colonial America from 1690 to 1715, long after the Pilgrims settled. Ask the children to discuss what they already know about life in early America.

Background information for this book is presented as letters and diary entries of the Cavendish family. Read Humility's first letter on page 5 to the class. Discuss the language in the letter. People were much more formal with one another than they are today. Discuss any words they do not understand. Repeat this when you read other letters. For younger children you may want to tape the letters onto a cassette so that they can listen to them as they start new activities. The Cavendish family will provide your class with a wealth of information about how people lived in colonial times. All the materials you will need for the lessons are included. However, if questions arise, refer to the bibliography.

Using the Activities in This Book

The purpose of this book is two-fold:
- to provide rich information on the day-to-day lives of Colonial Americans
- to organize easy-to-follow guidelines for using cooperative learning techniques in your classroom

If you are unfamiliar with cooperative techniques, see the appendix in the back of the book for pointers and for a more detailed key to the recipe symbols shown with each lesson. Cooperative symbols at the beginning of each activity will tell you how to organize groups and how they will proceed. Beside the symbols social skills, academic skills and teacher directions are provided.

See the appendix in the back of the book for:
- Cooperative learning overview and classroom guidelines
- Social skill descriptions and teaching techniques
- Cooperative recipe descriptions and symbols
- Reproducible classroom management charts and role badges
- Reproducible reward certificate

Chapter 1: Challenges in a New World

February 14, 1690

My Dearest Aunt Constance,

This may be the last letter you receive from me in many a month. My heart aches every time I think of our last farewell to you several weeks ago in London. Now we are only separated by a few miles of land. Soon we will be separated by the vast distance of the Atlantic Ocean. We will probably never set eyes on each other again. Mr. Cavendish and I still believe that our life in the New World will be a better one than we could ever have in England. We will own land of our own and raise Caleb and Abigail there. We could never have our own land here. The towns are so crowded that my husband would have hardly a chance to provide food and a home for us. So, with a heavy heart, but much hope for the future, we are bound for the New World.

So much has happened since we left you. Mr. Cavendish, the children and I are still in London awaiting the departure of our sailing ship, the Godspeed . We have bought supplies for our first few months in the colony. We are allowed only four trunks for all our worldly belongings. There have been many hard choices. I had to sell the fine lace table linens you gave us on our wedding day. They have been replaced by one trunkful of sturdy clothes that will last us a long while. Our bed, chest of drawers, table and one chair, and cooking utensils, tools and firearms and powder are already stowed below deck. Captain Howard says we must take money, apparel, farm tools, seed and animals. The animals will be stored below deck for the long voyage. We bought a cow, two sheep and two pigs to start our farm. Captain Howard assures us we will never make it on our own if we can not discipline ourselves to diligence and hard work. I am a little afraid of what is to come, but my husband, Mr. Cavendish, has great hopes for opportunities. This is overwhelming to those of us who have had no hope before.

We have met some of the people with whom we shall set sail. Many also are plowmen seeking land of their own and independence. Others are being indentured to land owners. They will work for a number of years and be given land of their own to farm when they are done. Others are not welcome in England unless they worship as they are told. Mr. Cavendish met some rather roguish men in the tavern who are going to the New World for adventure. He says they will have to find a trade to live there. He says no one can survive on dreams alone.

We will be setting sail after the ship is loaded with our provisions. There is word that there have been several storms at sea of late. From what I have heard, the voyage may be the worst of our ordeal to come. Pray for us, dearest aunt. I will write you again when the voyage is done. The captain will see that our letters are posted when he returns to England.

Your loving niece,
Humility

April 17, 1690 Diary of Caleb Cavendish, age 8

Our family arrived in Philadelphia at long last. Fair winds and weather favored our voyage for some days. Once out on the rolling waters of the Atlantic, alone in a vast world of sky and water, the weather suddenly changed. A terrible storm arose. Mighty waves rolled across the decks. All the passengers were below deck hovered in their bunks with fear and seasickness. I thought surely we would perish, but the captain remained calm as the ship tossed in the water. The Godspeed was a strong ship and plowed bravely through the heaving waters. One man, a Mister Jones, ventured up on deck and was washed into the sea. Luckily, he grabbed a topsail rope and the sailors were able to haul him aboard. He did not go on the deck again until we caught sight of land.

The passenger cabin was very crowded. There was no place to bathe or wash clothes. Our provisions were adequate, but we reduced our rations because the storm threw us off course and the voyage took longer than expected. We ate mostly hard bread and cheese and occasionally smoked fish and dried beef. There was not much for children to do on board. When the seas were calm, we went down in the hold to see the animals or walked up and down on deck.

Finally, two days ago we spotted land at last and thanked the Good Lord for our safe passage to Philadelphia. We will be leaving this growing town for our land as soon as we have all our belongings off the ship. One adventure has ended with our arrival. Now a new one begins with the clearing of our land and building of our home.

April 17, 1690 Diary of Joseph Cavendish

The ship has at last landed in America. Through divine providence, our family is well and healthy. Little Abigail had a terrible seasickness on the voyage. But her mother and I believe she is fine now that we are on land again. The first stop I made here in Philadelphia was at the blacksmith shop. The owner sold me a pair of oxen to pull our wagon. As soon as it is loaded we will depart.

There are no roads outside of town. We will drive the oxen through the woods and across streams to get to our land. It will be another hard journey of at least a week. How we are blessed to be able to build our own farm in this vast wilderness.

Some poor families are not so well off as we. They thought they would be able to get almost everything they would need here to start a farm. They will have to make many tools themselves before they can start to clear the land and plant crops. I have promised to lend ours to our new neighbor to help him get started. We will clear our lands together and do the best that we can. Our first job will be to build shelter to protect us from the spring rains. It will not be much of a house at first, but I shall build a better one when the crops are planted.

Social Skills: Work toward a goal, summarize, elaborate.
Academic Skill: Understand and list reasons colonists came to America.
Teacher: Reproduce one *Ship Word Web* sheet for each group.

WHY THEY CAME

Why did people come to Colonial America? Take turns writing your answers on each sail.

Ship Word Web

Extending Activity: REASONS Round Robin
Reorganize groups to discuss similar or different opinions.

Social Skills: Speak clearly, listen actively, paraphrase.
Academic Skill: Knowing necessary supplies needed for a life in a new country.
Teacher: Ask children to orally list the things colonists would need for living in America.

WHAT THEY BROUGHT AND WHY

Discuss in your group all the things you would need to bring to the New World to survive.

Social Skills: Use names, seek accuracy, work toward a goal.
Academic Skill: Identify where colonial implements go in an interior and exterior setting.
Teacher: Enlarge or trace the trunk pattern onto brown paper for a bulletin board.
Note: Use this bulletin board in the "Land Ho" activity on page 16.

PACK IT UP

Work with a partner. Draw pictures of the things you would pack for a journey to America. Tack them in and around the trunk on the bulletin board.

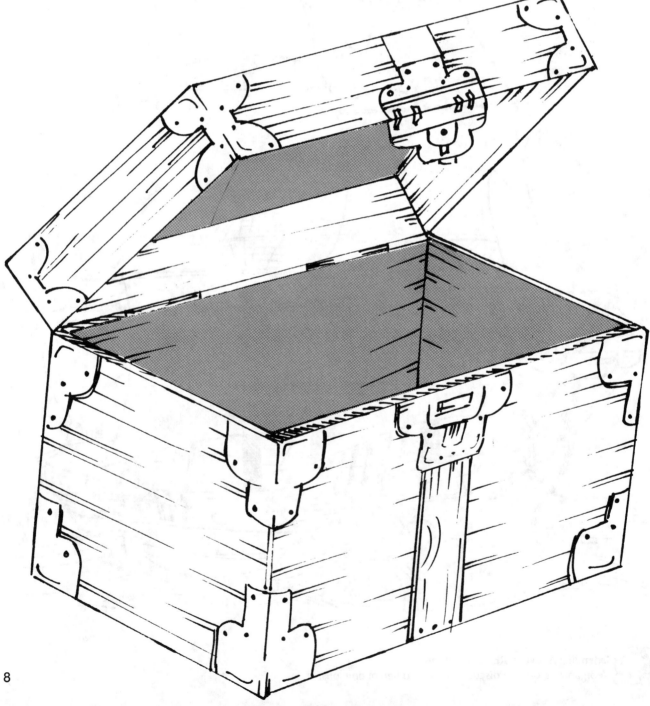

Social Skills: Speak clearly, listen actively, no put-downs.
Academic Skill: To imagine and tell in words and movements a tale of an ocean voyage.
Teacher: Give each student in a group a different *Story Starter Strip*.

OUR DIFFICULT JOURNEY

Use your Story Starter Strips to write a story about your ocean voyage to America. Combine the stories in your round-robin group to describe all the events of the voyage.

Story Starter Strips

We are so homesick. I don't know many people on this ship except family.
The ship is so crowded. We have to sleep three to a bunk.
We have not changed clothes or bathed for days. There is not enough fresh water.
The ship rocks and bobbles in the ocean. Everyone is getting seasick.
We have to eat dried food. There is no place for all of us to cook.
The terrible stormy winds are blowing water across the deck. We are so frightened.
Water, water everywhere, will we ever see land again?
Walking on deck can be dangerous. We could lose our balance and fall overboard.

Extending Activity 1: TEAM SHARE stories
Groups take their stories "on the road" to tell and act out for others.

Extending Activity 2 : Study Group STORY STARTERS
Develop more *Story Starter Strips* to exchange with other groups.

Social Skills: Participate, no put-downs, seek accuracy.
Academic Skill: Recognize and remember details of a trip at sea.
Teacher: Reproduce one *Picture Study Sheet* for each pair to complete.

ON THE BOUNDING MAIN

Look at the picture with your partner. List the hardships you might encounter on a sea voyage.

Picture Study Sheet

A Colonial Sea Voyage

Social Skills: Seek accuracy, ask questions, integrate a number of ideas.
Academic Skill: Recognize and complete the interior of a ship of the colonial period.
Teacher: Reproduce one set of cargo stickers and ship pieces for each group.

WORKING ABOARD SHIP

Work together to learn about ships in colonial times. Cut out all the cargo stickers. Cut out the ship pieces and glue them together. Glue on cargo stickers to load the ship.

Cargo Stickers

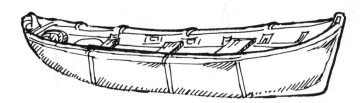

Working Aboard Ship Piece 1

Cut out the two ship pieces and glue them together as shown. Add cargo stickers from page 11 to load the ship's cargo.

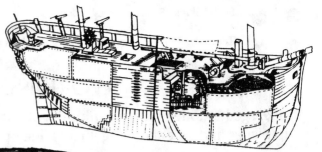

GLUE HERE

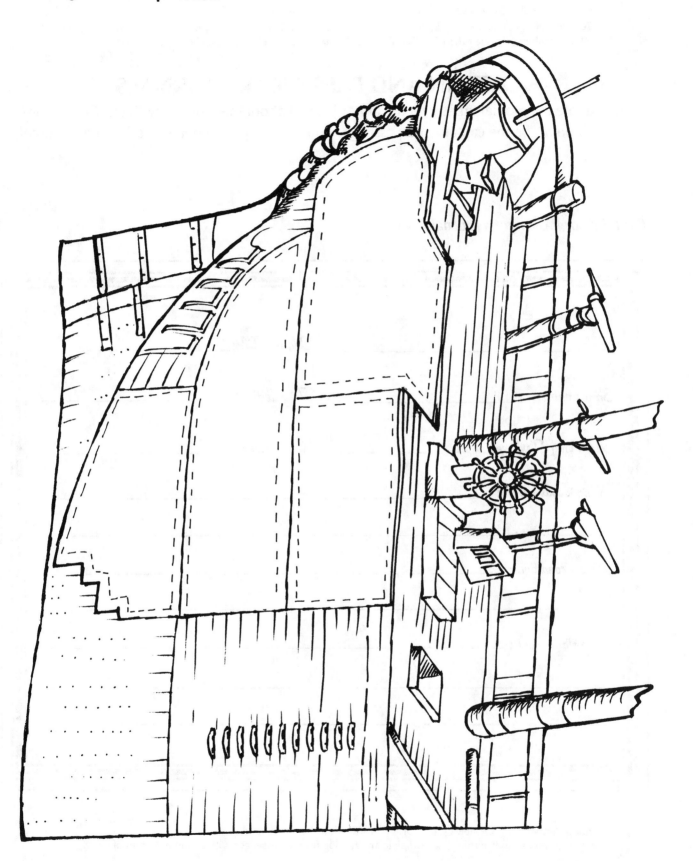

Extending Activity: SHIP-SHAPE classroom display
Use the *Work Aboard Ship* patterns to make a larger ship outline on butcher paper for a bulletin board. Students add colorful details.

Social Skills: Listen actively, paraphrase.

Academic Skill: Discuss and record events of a typical ocean voyage.

Teacher: Reproduce one *Log/Journal Fill-In* for each group. Use the role buttons from the appendix to have the other members take the roles of RECORDER, TASK MASTER and ENCOURAGER (see page 109).

CAPTAIN AND PASSENGER JOURNALS

Many people in colonial times kept a diary or journal about their everyday lives. Choose one team member to be the captain or a passenger on board ship. Interview and fill in the journal.

Captain's or Passenger's Journal Fill-in

Date: _____

Name, Title: _____

Ship's name: _____

My destination: _____

How long I've been at sea: _____

The weather today: _____

What foods we eat: _____

_____

Living conditions: _____

_____

Important events: _____

_____

_____

_____

Extending Activity: ANOTHER POINT OF VIEW Interview
Teams may want to switch roles and complete another log from a passenger with a different point of view.

Extending Activity: TRIP TO A NEW WORLD Team Share
Tack the completed logs up around your trunk bulletin board. Invite other classes to come and read them. Have team members answer questions about their logs.

May 13, 1690

Dear Aunt Constance,

I am taking this opportunity to write to you because our new neighbor, Mr. John Griffin, is traveling to Philadelphia and will see that this letter is posted to you in England. He did not know that he should bring everything he would need to survive in this absolute wilderness. He will have to trade most of his household goods to get seed and farming tools in order to be able to grow enough food to preserve for the winter. Joseph is helping as much as he can by letting him use our oxen to clear the trees away for growing fields. We are so thankful that he read about the other settlers and learned that everyone must be self-sufficient to live here.

Wildlife abounds in the forests and rivers on our land. There are berries growing wild and there will be walnuts from the trees in the autumn. The trees are more plentiful and larger than any I saw in England. Joseph and Caleb have cleared an area for our first planting. We are living in a small shelter made of bark walls and a thatched roof. I cook over an open fire outside. Joseph and Caleb will build us a proper house with the help of the neighbors after the crops are planted. We have everything we need for now, but must prepare for winter.

Life in America is quite different from England. There are no shops out here to buy what we need. We have to make everything ourselves. All the new settlers are busy making a home for themselves and have no excess goods to trade. Flax has been planted so that I will be able to spin and weave linen in the autumn. We have enough clothes for now, but Abigail is growing so fast that she will need more very soon. We have also planted corn, pumpkins, beans and a few apple and cherry trees. The only things we trade for are powder for the musket, sugar and flour. Flour is so expensive that we use mainly cornmeal for our bread. We eat corn in some manner at every meal.

The children and Joseph send their love. This letter may not reach you for some months, so we will take the time to wish you a Merry Christmas. You may be surprised to hear that we will be celebrating the arrival of a new baby here in America at Christmas. You may write to us at the Crooked Billet Inn on Water Street in Philadelphia. Joseph made friends with the proprietor there and he will see that any letters get to us.

Your loving niece,

Humility

Social Skills: Form groups quietly, use quiet voices, vocalize.
Academic Skill: Understanding necessities needed for survival in America, categorizing.
Teacher: Reproduce enough *Wilderness Condition Cards* so that each group can have one card.

LAND HO! ARRIVING IN THE NEW WORLD

Work in your study groups to develop a list of food, clothing and tools you would need to bring from England to start life in the New World. When your list is complete, pick a Wilderness Condition Card to compare to your list. Did you bring everything you needed?

Wilderness Condition Cards

You have landed in a swampy marshland. You will need to travel inland to build your home and plant crops on solid ground.	*You have landed on a windy plain. You will need to build temporary shelter to protect your family from the elements.*
You have landed on a barren, rocky shore. You will need to move the big stones and build your first shelters with them.	*You have arrived in a thickly forested area. You will need to clear rough terrain to plant crops and to build a home.*

Shopping List for England

To: *Milton Charles, Esq.*
Purchasing Agent, London, England
From: _____
Address: _____

_____

_____

_____

_____

_____

_____

_____

Extending Activity: SHOPPING LIST TO ENGLAND
Reproduce one *shopping list form* for each group to complete to order the supplies they determined were needed from the activity above.

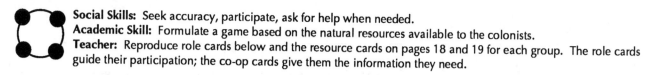

Social Skills: Seek accuracy, participate, ask for help when needed.
Academic Skill: Formulate a game based on the natural resources available to the colonists.
Teacher: Reproduce role cards below and the resource cards on pages 18 and 19 for each group. The role cards guide their participation; the co-op cards give them the information they need.

LAND OF PLENTY GAMES AND ACTIVITIES

Colonists found many natural resources available in the New World. Use the Resource Co-Op Cards to plan your own game or puzzle. The role cards will help you. Share your game.

Land of Plenty Role Cards

Role 1:
Pick ten resource cards.
Choose a variety of animal,
vegetable and land resources.

Role 3:
Create a puzzle or game
using all ten cards.

Tips: It can be a trail game, hidden word puzzle, picture game or any activity of your design.

Role 2:
Sort into animal, vegetable
and land resources.

Role 4:
Write game directions.
Play it with your group.

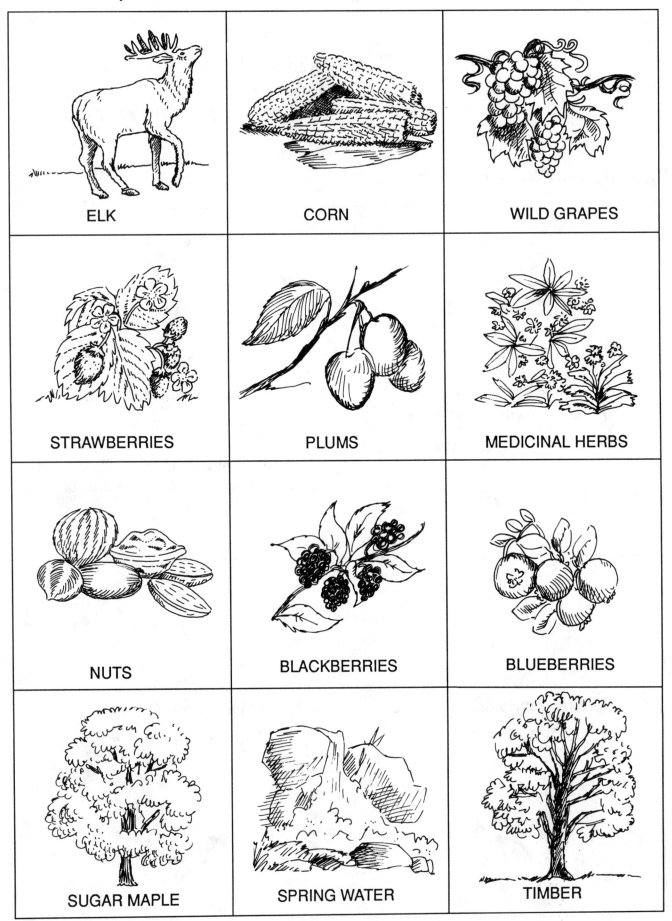

ELK

CORN

WILD GRAPES

STRAWBERRIES

PLUMS

MEDICINAL HERBS

NUTS

BLACKBERRIES

BLUEBERRIES

SUGAR MAPLE

SPRING WATER

TIMBER

DUCK

GOOSE

WILD TURKEY

DEER

SQUIRREL

RABBIT

FISH

LOBSTER

EEL

PHEASANT

BUILDING STONES

SHRIMP

September 25, 1688 Diary of Caleb Cavendish

Yesterday we moved into our new little house. Father and I spent spare days in the summer cutting trees and sawing them into boards and timbers for the walls. He cut cedar into shingles for the roof while I gathered stones for the fireplace. After the fireplace was built, we built the frame for the walls on the ground. All the neighbors from miles around came to help us with the house-raising. What fun to have friends with us. All the men and boys worked all day putting up the frame and hammering on the boards for the walls. All the women cooked food and made ready for the evening celebration. After the work was done, we had a huge feast, played games and danced to Mr. Griffin's fiddle playing. It was a wonderful day.

Tonight I am sitting by the fire in our one-room house. It is much appreciated after spending the summer sleeping on the ground in our little hut. Father and I have made a few pieces of furniture to make our house more comfortable. My next project is to carve a pretty design into the cradle that Father is building for the new baby.

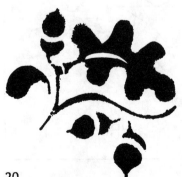

Social Skills: Plan out loud, no put-downs, seek accuracy.
Academic Skill: Complete a diorama of a colonial homestead.
Teacher: Reproduce the *Diorama Cutouts* on pages 21 and 22 for each group. Provide each group with a box.

GETTING READY FOR WINTER

Make a diorama of the house-raising you read about in Caleb's diary. Color the illustrations. Cut them out. Fold back the tabs so that they stand inside a box. Add your own drawings or natural materials like sticks or leaves.

Diorama Cutouts

Extending Activity: Team Share DIORAMAS
Teams describe what personal touches were added to their displays and why.

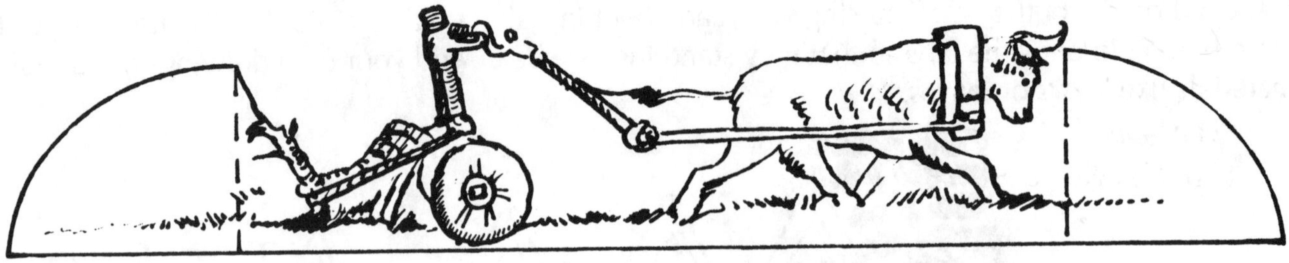

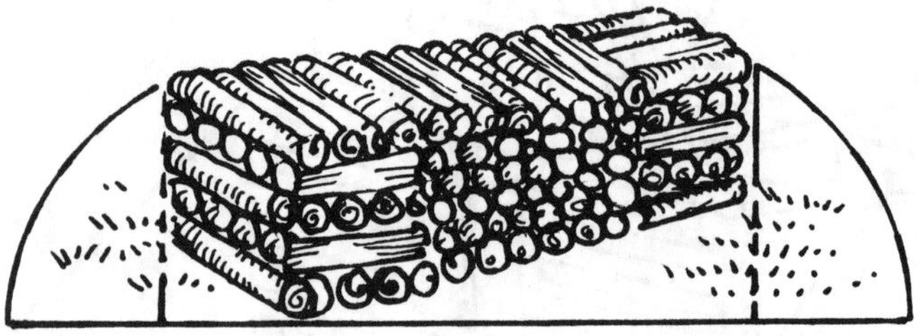

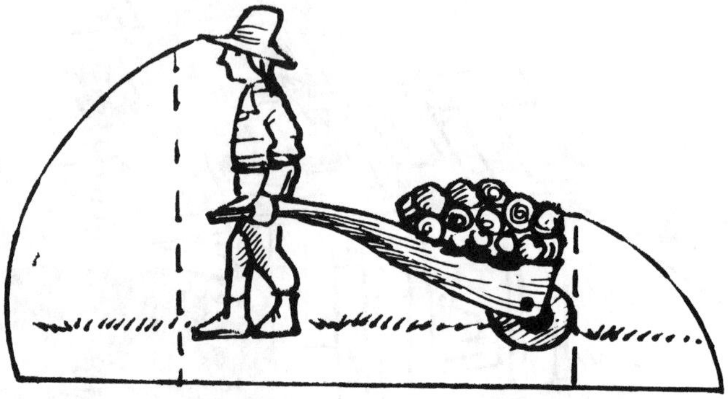

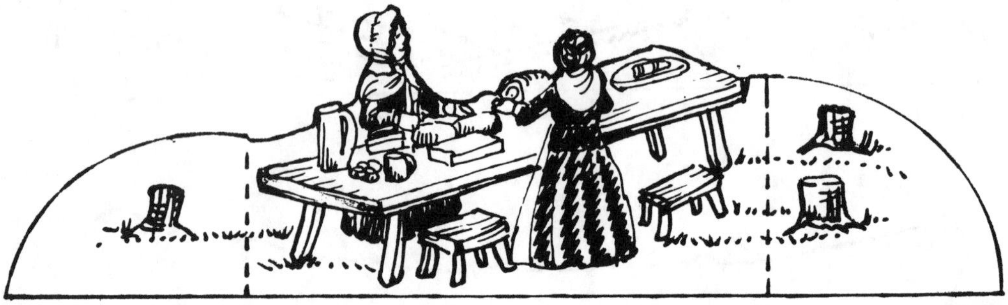

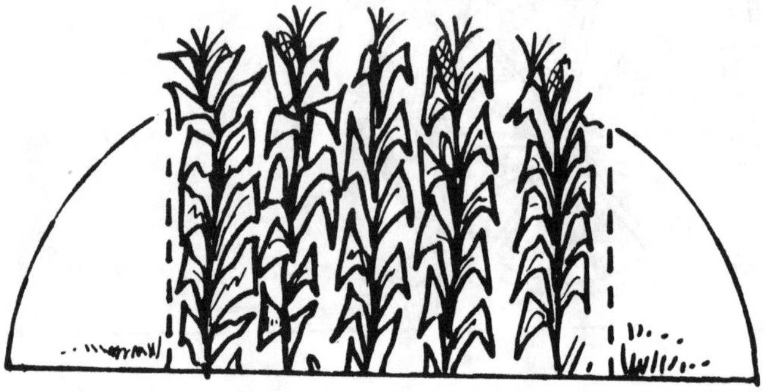

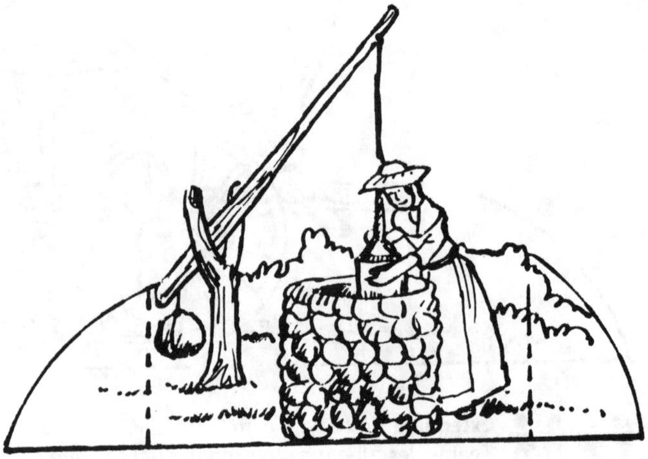

Chapter 2: Home and Hearth

September 3, 1698 Diary of Abigail Cavendish

 Today is my twelfth birthday. I rose at first light as usual. After helping Mother with breakfast and getting the twins, Constance and Jacob, dressed, I spun two pounds of flax, scoured the kettles, made cheese, ironed tablecloths and napkins and sanded the floor.* I assembled the quilting frame and moved all the chairs around it.

 In the afternoon Mother had a quilting bee for my birthday. All the neighbor ladies had made squares. The afternoon was spent stitching the squares together and sewing them to the backing. We gossiped and laughed as we sewed. After the quilt was finished, Mother and I served cake and cider. What a beautiful quilt! It is in my hope chest for the day when I marry and start a home with my husband. Father reminded me that that would be several years away. Mother laughed and said our days are so busy that years pass very quickly.

*Note: In lieu of rugs, colonial families spread a thin layer of fine, clean sand on the floor.

September 3, 1698
Dear Aunt Constance,

 The Cavendish family is well and prospering. The twins are four now and a great help to us. Constance helps with carding wool. She can piece a quilt together nicely. Jacob helps in the fields and weeds the herb garden. Abigail is a great help. She spins flax and is a very neat housekeeper. She is becoming quite a seamstress as well. Miles is eight. He helps me get the fire going in the morning and chops all the firewood. Caleb is a man of sixteen. He is quite talented in woodworking. We are very proud of the furniture he has made for us.

 Our family is never idle. The children have chores to do every day. There are soap and candles to make, wool and linen to weave as well as keeping the house clean and food on the table. By necessity we have learned how to fix things and to make do with what we have. I am even learning to cure ills with herbs and roots.

 We have bright, happy moments in the evenings. The children sit by the fireplace scraping corn from cobs or knitting mittens. Joseph is still a great storyteller. Young Constance's favorite is "Jack and the Beanstalk." Abigail still loves "Tom Thumb." We listen and laugh at the stories as we work. Later we enjoy a treat of roasted apples or popcorn and cider. Life is busy here and we are content. We so enjoy your letters from England. They generally arrive by post rider in about three months.

       Your loving niece,
       Humility

Social Skills: Use quiet voices, jog memory of teammate.
Academic Skill: Learn the names and uses of colonial implements.
Teacher: Reproduce the cards on pages 24--27 for each pair. They may not be familiar with the vocabulary. See the bibliography on page 111 for assistance.

PARTNERS FLASH CARDS

Cut the cards apart. Look at each picture. How do you think each tool is used? Discuss the words on the cards. Look in the dictionary or other reference books for words you don't know.

Indoor Tools Co-Op Cards

Extending Activity: COLONIAL CONCENTRATION GAME
Put two pairs together and use both sets of cards to play a concentration memory game. Mix the cards. Place them face down in rows. Partners take turns revealing two cards. If they match, they tell if the tool is used inside or outside the home. Paired cards are put into a pile. The game is over when all cards have been paired.

PIGGIN	WOODEN BARREL	WOODEN BUCKET
CHURN	**WOODEN MUG, TRENCHER AND SPOONS**	**WOODEN TANKARD**
PEWTER PORRINGER **SALT CELLAR**	**CAST IRON TEA KETTLE AND TRIVET**	**PEWTER SPOON MOLD AND SPOON**
CAST IRON POT	**SPINNING WHEEL**	**SUGAR CUTTER**

SETTLE	JACK AND TRUNDLE BEDS	TRESTLE TABLE
CARVER CHAIR	CHEST OF DRAWERS	CRADLE
CLOTHING PEGS	STOOL	BENCH
TRUNK	LINEN CHEST	ROCKING CHAIR

Outdoor Tools Co-Op Cards

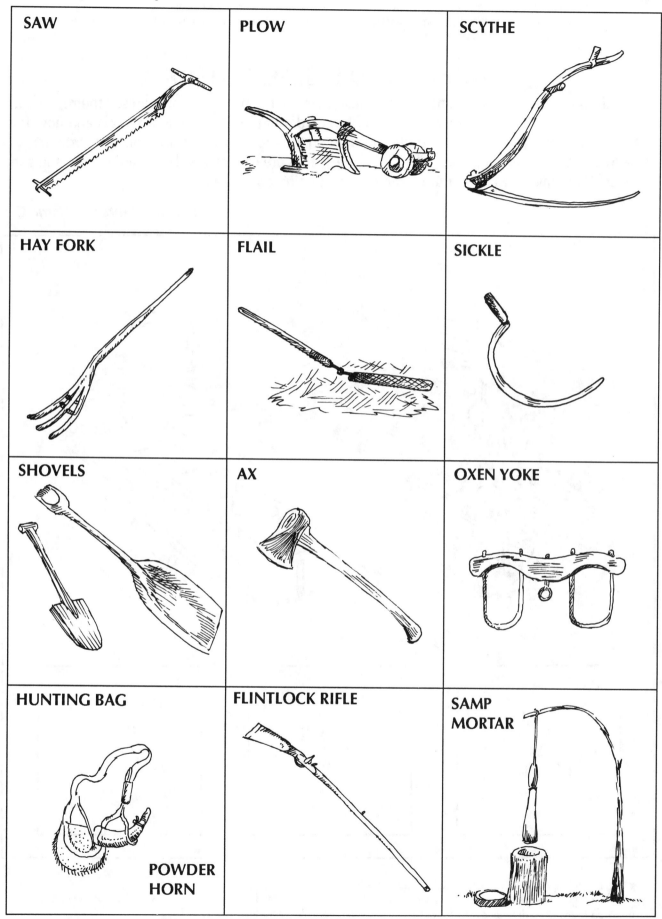

SAW

PLOW

SCYTHE

HAY FORK

FLAIL

SICKLE

SHOVELS

AX

OXEN YOKE

HUNTING BAG

POWDER HORN

FLINTLOCK RIFLE

SAMP MORTAR

Social Skills: Use names, seek accuracy, work toward a goal.
Academic Skill: Identify where colonial implements go in an interior and exterior setting.
Teacher: Reproduce the *Game Cards* on pages 28 and 29. Teams use them with the furnishings/utensils and tools co-op cards to play a simple game.

HOMESTEAD INSIDE/OUTSIDE

Directions: Play with both game cards. Place them so that both partners can see them. Turn all co-op cards face down. Partner 1 picks a co-op card. Partner 2 explains what it is and how it is used. If partner 1 agrees, partner 2 puts it down on the proper game card space. If partner 1 disagrees, the card is put back. When all three spaces are covered on both game cards, the game is over. You may play another time using the remaining co-op cards.

Homestead Interior Game Card

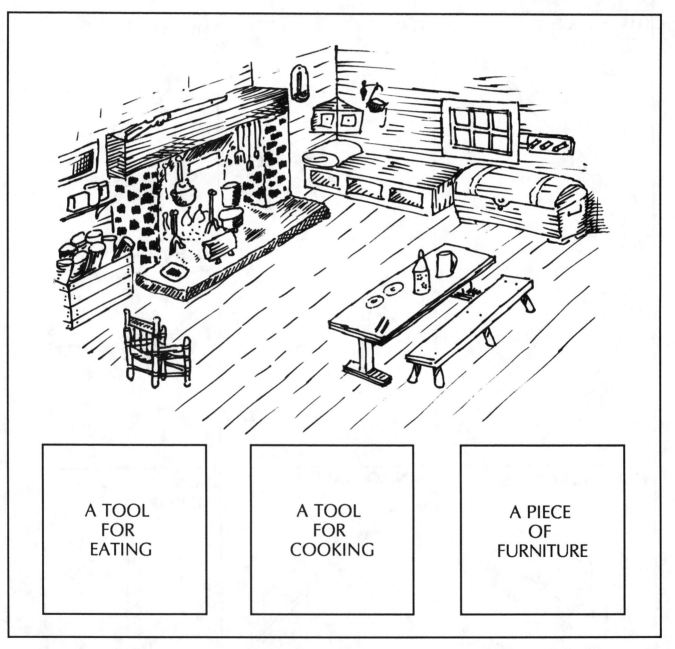

A TOOL FOR EATING	A TOOL FOR COOKING	A PIECE OF FURNITURE

Extending Activity: COLONIAL HOMESTEAD Bulletin Board
Enlarge a *Homestead Card* from page 28 or 29 to create a homestead bulletin board. Assign the groups items from the co-op cards to draw or color, cut out and add to complete the homestead scene.

| A TOOL FOR FARMING | A TOOL FOR HUNTING | A TOOL FOR BUILDING |

Social Skills: Seek accuracy, use quiet voices, ask for help if needed
Academic Skill: Follow steps to re-create a colonial recipe.
Teacher: Reproduce the recipe for each pair. Gather all the materials. Be sure teams are closely supervised, especially with the embroidery needles. They are duller than regular needles.

DRYING FOOD FOR WINTER

Follow the steps on the recipe card to learn about preserving food. Bring in other dried fruits or vegetables to share in discussions with the class.

Pairs Check Recipe Card

Tools:	**To Make:**
string	Partners take turns getting tools and ingredients and following each step of the recipe. Check off each task as it is completed.
embroidery needles	
knife	
lidded storage container	1. Cut apples in slices. Cut out core.
	2. Thread the apple slices onto string.
Ingredient:	3. Hang in a sunny spot to dry for about 8-12 hours. Apples will be dry on the outside, but moist on the inside.
fresh apples	5. Store in containers with tight-fitting lids.
Note: Choose apples that are firm, with no bruises.	

Social Skills: Seek accuracy, participate, ask for help if needed.
Academic Skill: Follow steps to re-create a colonial recipe.
Teacher: Gather necessary materials. Children should be closely supervised during the cooking.

CORN PUDDIN'

Each member of your study group should have a part in making this recipe.

Study Group Recipe Card

Tools:	**To Make:**
saucepan	One teammate gathers tools; another, ingredients. Read over the recipe carefully. Decide on each team member's tasks.
measuring cups and spoon	
egg beater	
shallow baking dish	1. Preheat oven to 350º. Grease baking dish with a little butter.
toaster oven at 350º	2. Melt butter in saucepan. Add flour and stir until blended.
Ingredients:	3. Slowly stir in corn liquid and cream mixture.
2 Tbsp. each butter and flour	4. Stir until smooth and hot. Add the drained corn and boil.
2 1/2 cups canned corn	5. Reduce heat to low. Stir some corn mixture into the egg yolks.
Corn liquid and cream to equal 1 cup	6. Add mixture to rest of corn. Stir three minutes. Add salt.
2 egg yolks	7. Beat egg whites until stiff. Stir them gently into the corn mixture.
3/4 tsp. salt	
2 egg whites, beaten	

 **Social Skills:** Seek accuracy, use quiet voices, ask for help if needed.
Academic Skill: Follow steps to re-create a colonial recipe.

HOE CAKES

Hoe cakes were prepared on plantations and cooked on a hoe over an open fire. This recipe has been updated to be baked in an oven.

Pairs Check Recipe Card

Tools:	To Make:
measuring cup and spoons mixing bowl and spoon cookie sheet **Ingredients:** 1 cup corn meal 1 1/2 tsp. salt 1/2 cup milk 1 Tbsp. butter 1/2 tsp. baking powder Boiling water	One partner gets tools; the other, ingredients. One partner mixes ingredients while the other follows directions and checks off each step. 1. Preheat oven to 325º. Grease cookie sheet with a little butter. 2. Mix all ingredients except boiling water in a bowl. Stir. 3. Stir in boiling water a little at a time to make a stiff batter. 4. Roll in small balls. Place on cookie sheet and flatten slightly. 5. Bake for 30 minutes. Allow to cool before eating.

Social Skills: Seek accuracy, use quiet voices, ask for help if needed.
Academic Skill: Follow steps to re-create a colonial recipe.

APPLESAUCE

Apples were prepared in many of the same ways we enjoy them today.

Pairs Check Recipe Card

Tools:	To Make:
knife measuring spoon stirring spoon electric crock pot **Ingredients:** 1 lb. Jonathan, Winesap or McIntosh apples 1 cup hot water 1/2 cup sugar or to taste 1 Tbl. cinnamon or to taste 2 tsp. lemon juice	One partner gets tools and ingredients. The other cuts the apples. Both watch the sauce as it cooks and stir occasionally. Prepare early in the school day and enjoy in the afternoon. 1. Wash the apples. Cut them into quarters. Cut out cores. 2. Add apples to crock pot. 3. Add rest of ingredients. 4. Put on lid. Turn crock pot to high. 5. Stir occasionally. Add sugar or cinnamon, if necessary. 6. Cook about five hours.

Social Skills: Seek accuracy, use quiet voices, ask for help if needed.
Academic Skill: Follow steps to re-create a colonial recipe.
Teacher: Reproduce recipe. Be sure children are closely supervised while handling the hot cider.

MULLED CIDER

Colonial families drank lots of cider. This recipe was a favorite on cold, wintry nights.

Pairs Check Recipe Card

Tools:	**To Make:**
large saucepan stirring spoon mugs	One partner gets tools and ingredients. The other mixes ingredients. Both help each other check each step.
Ingredients: 1/2 gallon apple cider a few cloves cinnamon stick a few allspice berries	1. Pour cider into saucepan. 2. Add rest of ingredients. 3. Heat until hot, but not boiling. 4. Pour into mugs and serve.

Social Skills: Seek accuracy, use quiet voices, ask for help if needed.
Academic Skill: Follow steps to re-create a colonial recipe.
Teacher: Watch children closely. Be sure the candy is cool enough to handle before shaping patties.

MAPLE CANDY

Men and boys from several families often made a party of gathering maple sap in early spring. They boiled it down into syrup right in the forest.

Pairs Check Recipe Card

Tools:	**To Make:**
sauce pan mixing spoon candy thermometer storage tin	One partner gets tools; the other, ingredients. One mixes ingredients; one uses candy thermometer. Both help make the candy patties. 1. Cook syrup over very low heat until boiling. 2. Boil until temperature reaches 233º on candy thermometer.
Ingredients: 2 cups pure maple syrup 1 tsp. vanilla	3. Remove from heat and cool to 110º, about an hour. 4. Add vanilla and beat until smooth and fluffy. 5. Shape into small patties. Put into storage tin immediately to avoid candy drying out.

Extending Activity: COLONIAL FOOD FEST Team Share
Bring in other colonial recipes to share. Set them aside to include in the almanac activities later in the book.

Social Skills: Work toward a goal, integrate a number of ideas, no put-downs.
Academic Skill: Follow steps to re-create a colonial craft.
Teacher: Help children gather materials. Younger children will need help in assembly.

A LOOM TO CRAFT

Loom Pairs Check Directions

Materials:
4 6" pieces 1"-thick wood
20 nails
ruler
pencil
hammer
heavy string

To Make:
1. Stack wood in a square as shown.
2. Nail together at the four corners.
3. Use ruler and pencil to mark 1/2" intervals on two opposite sides of the frame.
4. Hammer nails into each mark, leaving about 1/4" above the frame as shown.
5. Tie end of heavy string to one corner nail. Wind string across the frame around first two nails on the opposite side. Continue winding across the loom to the last nail. Tie a knot and cut the string.

WE-WEAVE

Round Table Weaving Directions

Materials:
loom
weaving materials:
    bulky yarn, ribbon,
    straw, long grass,
    reeds
pan of water to soak
natural materials
scissors
needle
heavy thread

To Make:
1. Team members each choose weaving materials and cut them in lengths 4" longer than the width of the loom. Natural materials should be soaked in water to make them pliable.
2. To weave, use one strand of material. Go over the first string and under the next. Continue to opposite side of loom. Push weaving material up close to the nails.
3. Pass the loom to the next person to weave one strand. Be sure to push pieces close together to make a tight weave. Continue weaving and passing loom until the loom is full.
4. When loom is full, gently lift the weaving off the loom.
5. Sew along both edges to keep the weaving from raveling. Trim uneven edges, if you like.

Social Skills: No put-downs, work toward a goal, integrate ideas.
Academic Skill: Create a play and complete steps to color and cut out a colonial character.
Teacher: Reproduce *Script Starters* and *Script Fill-Ins* for each group. Each child picks one starter. Groups use their *Script Starters* to produce a short play. Reproduce character puppets on tagboard from pages 36-39.

COLONIAL FAMILY PLAYS

Each member of your group chooses one script starter. Make up a short play using the Cavendish family puppets. You may want to draw and color scenery or props.

Script Starters

A bear scratched at our door this morning.
The huge trout fought at the end of my line.
Abigail knew she could find her way out of the forest.
Constance and Jacob are making mischief in the garden.
Our family went to a barn-raising today.
The quilting bee was a huge success.
My father, Joseph, had an exciting time on the hunt.
Mr. Griffin brought us a surprise from Philadelphia.
We had to be in the house all day because of the storm.

Extending Activity: COLONIAL CAVALCADE
Teams give their puppet plays to other groups in class or classroom visitors.

Puppet Script Fill-In

Use with your *Script Starter* and puppets to write your play.

Play Title: —————————

Cast of Characters:

The Story:

Colonial Puppets

To Make the Puppets:
1. Choose the puppets you need for your play.
2. Color them with crayons or markers.
3. Cut out along the outlines.
4. Glue a wooden stick to the back of each puppet as shown in the diagram.
5. Write the puppet's name on its wooden stick.

Miles (age 8)

Abigail (age 12)

Constance (age 2)

Colonial Puppets

Teacher: Use characters for bulletin board scenes or for other activities as needed.

Humility

Joseph

Mr. Griffin

Mrs. Griffin

Abigail (age 17)

Constance (age 16)

Colonial Puppets

Jacob (age 20)

Miles (age 20)

Caleb (age 21)

Social Skills: Form groups quietly, participate, ask for help.
Academic Skill: Follow steps to re-create a colonial craft.
Teacher: Students go to their area of interest, then pair up to learn and complete the crafts. The materials lists below will help you get ready. Pairs check directions are included with craft patterns. Keep your crafts and projects on hand for the bartering exercises later.

COLONIAL CRAFTS

Graph Paper Sampler Materials List:
sampler pattern, page 41
1/4" graph paper
pencil
color pencils or fine-tip markers
construction paper for backing
quote strips from page 50

Quilting Squares List:
quilting patterns, page 44, reproduced on
     various colors of construction paper
tagboard for backing
scissors
glue or paste

Stenciling Materials List:
pineapple stencil pattern page, 42
tagboard for cutting stencil
small scissors
white tagboard for stenciling
masking tape
paints (red, yellow, brown, green)
brown paper bag
small pieces of fine sponge
glue or paste

Teacher: You may pre-cut stencils for younger students.

Candle-Making Materials List:
paraffin or old candle stubs
heavy string or candle wicking
pencils
small metal nuts
clean coffee can
saucepan
old crayons for dying wax (optional)
egg carton cut in half crossways
heat source

Papyrotamia Materials List
patterns, page 43
construction paper in two contrasting colors
scissors
glue or paste
masking tape

Soap-Whittling Materials List:
bar of soft soap
plastic knife

Extending Activity: CRAFT MAKER Roving Artisans
One member in each group teaches another group his or her craft "specialty."
Have extra materials ready for the artisans to take along.

GRAPH PAPER SAMPLER

Samplers showed how well a child knew how to sew. Learning to sew and embroider was necessary to making clothes, bed linens and napkins. Samplers usually had a short verse, the child's name and the date it was finished. A pretty border was usually added around the edge.

Directions: Partners take turns following and checking off each step.

1. Gather materials from materials list.
2. Choose a verse. Cut it out.
3. Turn the graph paper so the long edge faces you. Glue the verse to the center of the paper.
4. Use a pencil to X your initials at the top. Use the cross stitch letters below as a guide.
5. Use a pencil to add your initials at the bottom. Use the cross stitch letters as a guide.
6. Go over the Xs in your initials with color pencils or markers.
7. Add a decorative border where there is room at the top of the page.
8. Add a decorative border where there is room at the bottom of the page.
9. Glue your sampler to a piece of brightly colored construction paper.

Graph Paper Sampler Cross Stitch Letters, Numbers and Designs

[Cross stitch chart grid with letters, numbers and designs]

heart　　　　butterfly　　　　rabbit　　　　cat　　　　border　　　　border

STENCILING

Paint was scarce in colonial times. Stenciling used only a little paint. It became a popular way to decorate bare walls and furniture. The pineapple was a symbol of colonial hospitality.

Pineapple Stencil Pattern

Directions: Partners take turns following and checking off each step.

1. Gather all materials from the materials list.
2. Cut out the stencil pattern on the heavy black lines. Be careful in small areas.
3. Tape stencil in middle of white tagboard with pieces of masking tape.
4. Put a quarter-size drop of paint on brown paper bag.
5. Dip corner of sponge into paint. Dab on the bag to soak color into sponge.
6. Use a circular motion to rub paint lightly into open stencil areas.
7. Let stencil dry before changing colors.
8. Use another corner of the sponge when changing colors. Repeat same process.
9. When paint is dry, carefully remove tape and the stencil.

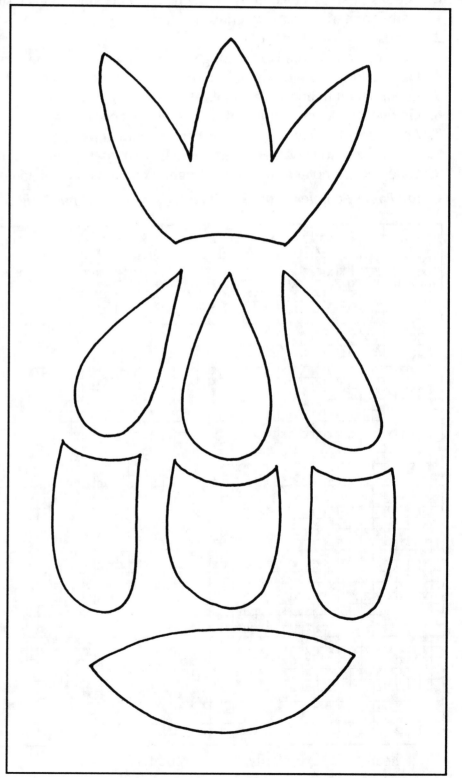

Teacher: Reproduce patterns on tagboard for each group.

PAPYROTAMIA

Paper was very expensive and scarce during colonial times. Every scrap was saved. On special occasions such as a wedding, a new baby or a birthday, gifts were made by cutting the paper into decorative designs. These gifts were cherished and kept for many years.

Directions: Partners take turns following and checking off each step.

1. Gather all materials from the materials list.
2. Fold one sheet of construction paper in half.
3. Tape the pattern to the construction paper. Be sure the fold line is on the fold of the construction paper.
4. Cut through the pattern and construction paper along the heavy black lines.
5. Carefully remove the pattern and tape. Unfold the design.
6. Glue design on a different color of construction paper.

Papyrotamia Patterns

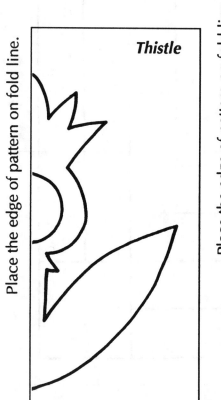

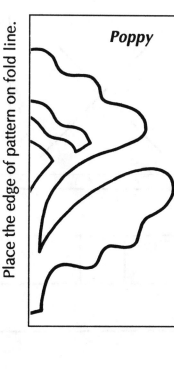

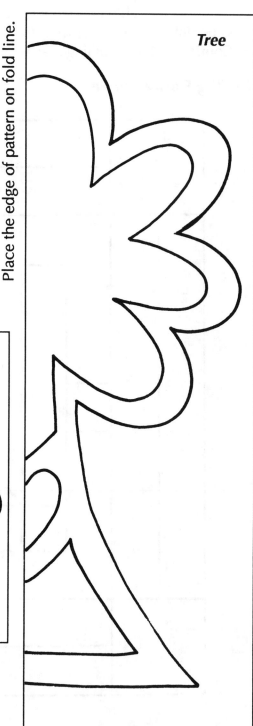

43

PAPER QUILTING

Quilting is considered an art today. In colonial times quilts were made into warm covers from scraps of cloth. You can follow the quilt pattern below or rearrange the pieces to make your own designs out of construction paper or printed gift wrap.

Directions:

1. Each team member takes a different color quilting square and a white quilt backing.
2. Cut apart the quilting square pieces. Pick out the pieces you need. Put the extras in the center of the table in separate piles so everyone can reach all the pieces.
3. Glue different quilting pieces to your quilt backing. Use pieces from the piles on the table.
4. Continue adding quilting pieces to your quilt backing until your design is finished.

Quilting Square Pattern

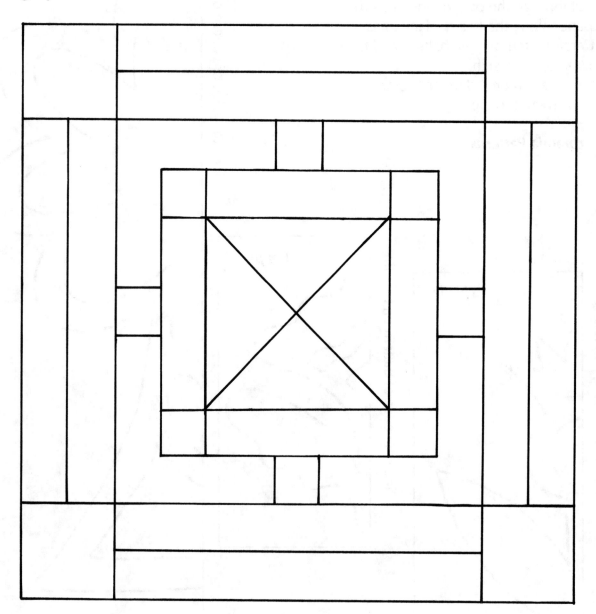

Social Skills: Stay in group, plan out loud, summarize.
Academic Skill: Follow steps to re-create a colonial craft.
Teacher: Organize materials for groups. Cut paraffin into 1/2" cubes. This activity should be closely supervised. Paraffin is flammable.

CLASSROOM CANDLE-MAKING

Candles were the main source of light in colonial homes. They were made at home in the fall from boiled animal fat or tallow.

Step 1: Preparing Materials	
Teammate 1: Gather candle materials. 13-oz. coffee can saucepan paraffin or old candle stubs wooden spoon potholder old crayons of one bright color	**Teammate 3:** Prepare pans. 1. Bend lip of coffee can to make a spout. 2. Put the coffee can in the saucepan. 3. Fill the can half full with paraffin pieces. 4. Fill the sauce pan two-thirds full with water.
Teammate 2: Gather and prepare mold. 1/2 plastic egg carton (6 compartments) 6 4" pieces candlewick or cotton string 2 pencils 6 small metal nuts •Tie three pieces of wicking to each pencil. •Tie nuts to wick ends as weights.	**Teammate 4:** Melt paraffin. 1. Place pan containing coffee can and paraffin over medium heat. 2. Heat until paraffin pieces are melted. 3. Use the spoon to stir in crayon pieces. 4. Turn off heat. 5. Use potholder to lift melted wax from pan.

Step 2: Making Candles	
Teammates 1 and 2: 1. Rest pencils on egg carton edges with one wick in each egg section. 2. Move wicks back and forth on the pencil so that they are centered in the egg sections. 3. Twist pencils until wicks hang straight.	**Teammates 3 and 4:** 1. Hold pencils steady over the mold. 2. Carefully pour melted paraffin into molds. 3. Set aside to harden. (about 1 hour) 4. Remove candles from carton and cut wicks to one-half inch.

Social Skills: Stay in group, plan out loud, summarize.
Academic Skill: Follow steps to re-create a colonial craft.
Teacher: Show children the whittling designs below or let them design one of their own. Be sure students keep their hands away from their eyes while whittling. Wash hands when done.

CLASSROOM SOAP WHITTLING

Directions: Pick a design from the samples shown below. Work together to plan and whittle the soap by passing it from person to person.

Note: Plastic knives can be quite sharp, so be careful! Use one side for texture, the other for smooth effects!

Soap Whittling Ideas

Extended Activity: WHITTLING BEE
Students sit and visit while whittling independently.

Chapter 3: Colonial Schools

There were few schools in Colonial America. Caleb, Abigail and the other children in the Cavendish family learned their letters and to read from their parents when they were very young. Later Mrs. Griffin at the next farm started a Dame School. Children would come to her kitchen each day to learn to read Bible verses and to recite lessons. They also learned to add and subtract. Lessons were often put into rhyme to make them easier to memorize. The poem "Thirty days hath September" was a typical lesson. Girls learned to mind their manners, to knit and to sew. A few learned to read, but it was not deemed as important as learning handiwork.

Mr. Cavendish made each child a hornbook to take to Dame School. It really was not a book at all, but a piece of paper with letters of the alphabet, a Bible verse or the Lord's Prayer. The pieces of paper were pasted to a small board and covered with thin pieces of horn that were almost transparent. Dutch people in New York made hornbook cookies from cookie molds. A child was permitted to eat the hornbook cookie as a reward for learning a lesson.

At about age seven some boys went to a grammar school. It was a cold and bleak one-room building. There were no blackboards or pictures on the walls. Boys sat on narrow, backless benches and recited lessons from memory. For at least eight hours a day boys had to sit quietly without fidgeting and write or recite monotonous lessons. If a boy made a mistake, he was whipped with a birch rod by the schoolmaster and told he was lazy or stupid. Other punishments included pinching the nose with a clothespin or balancing for a long period on one foot. Sometimes they had to sit in front of the class with a sign around their necks noting how they had misbehaved in class. The schoolmaster wrote lessons for children to copy and memorize each day. Boys wrote on pieces of birch bark with a piece of lead or a quill pen and ink. Handwriting was very important. Good penmanship was considered the sign of an educated person. There were spelling bees and recitations from the Bible. Being able to learn from the Bible was the main reason for learning to read.

Girls learned at home after they finished with Dame School. They excelled at handcrafts and homemaking. Handiwork and fancywork with beautiful embroidery or homemade lace were admired. Rich girls had private tutors who taught them to play a musical instrument or to sing. They also learned good manners, etiquette, dancing and dainty needlework.

Social Skills: Participate, no put-downs, seek accuracy.
Academic Skill: Learn calligraphic lettering techniques and quotations to recreate a colonial hornbook.
Teacher: Partners plan together to create a hornbook which contains a quote. Reproduce hornbook on tagboard or heavy tan paper for each team. The list of quotes is on page 50.

A COLONIAL HORNBOOK

Hornbooks were the only books most children had to learn to read and count.

A stitch in time saves nine.

Spare the rod and spoil the child.

Thirty days hath September,
April, June and November.
When short February is done,
All the rest have thirty one.

Directions: Partners work together.
1. Cut out the hornbook.
2. Both practice writing calligraphy letters.
3. Choose a quote from the list.
4. Write the quote on the back of the hornbook.

Teacher: This is a simplified calligraphy alphabet for your class to try. Follow the numbers and arrows to create each letter. For letters made in one continuous stroke, pause and change direction without picking up the pen. Your students may want to try it with a quill pen as shown below.

Calligraphy Alphabet

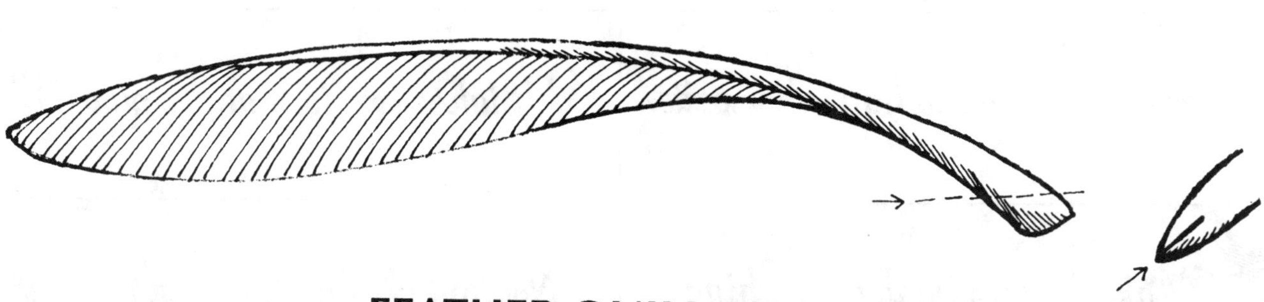

FEATHER QUILL PEN

Directions: Cut off the end of any large goose or turkey feather at a slant. Cut a small slit at the point. Dip in ink and use for calligraphy practice.

Teacher: Discuss the following quotations. Use them on the hornbook on page 48. Reproduce them for the almanac activity on page 53, the sampler activities on page 41 and the Schoolmaster Game on page 54.

Colonial Quotations Strips

Never put off until tomorrow what can be done today.	Birds of a feather flock together.
A place for everything and everything in its place.	Idleness is the mother of evil.
A rolling stone gathers no moss.	A new broom sweeps clean.
All that glitters is not gold.	God helps those who help themselves.
A fool and his money are soon parted.	Handsome is as handsome does.
Where there's a will, there's a way.	Two wrongs do not make a right.
The early bird catches the worm.	Curiosity killed the cat.
Everything comes to him who waits.	It takes two to make a quarrel.
Make hay while the sun shines.	Nothing ventured, nothing gained.

Social Skills: Integrate ideas, clarify, participate.
Academic Skills: Create a story and picture for letters of the alphabet.
Teacher: Assign a letter of the alphabet to each student. Pair students to make primer pages. Reproduce one primer spread for each pair. Assemble a classroom primer of the whole alphabet.

COLONIAL ABC's

After the hornbook, many children used small printed books called "primers."

Directions:
1. Think about your alphabet letter.
2. Partner one draws a picture for it on the primer page.
3. Partner two writes a verse or sentence using it. Switch roles for the right side of the page.

Primer Pages

Social Skills: Participate, seek accuracy, ask for help when needed.
Academic Skill: To represent colonial life in an almanac format.
Teacher: Students go to their area of interest to form study groups to find and share information to complete a section of a classroom almanac. Topics can include: **Weather, Recipes, Sayings, Farming Tips, Stories**, etc. Use the *Almanac Cover* and *Almanac Page* reproducibles. Decide on the categories you will want to include. Use other sources such as those listed in the bibliography or current almanacs for reference.

ALL-CLASS ALMANAC

Work together on one topic or research several. Assemble pages into a classroom book by adding the cover below.

Almanac Cover

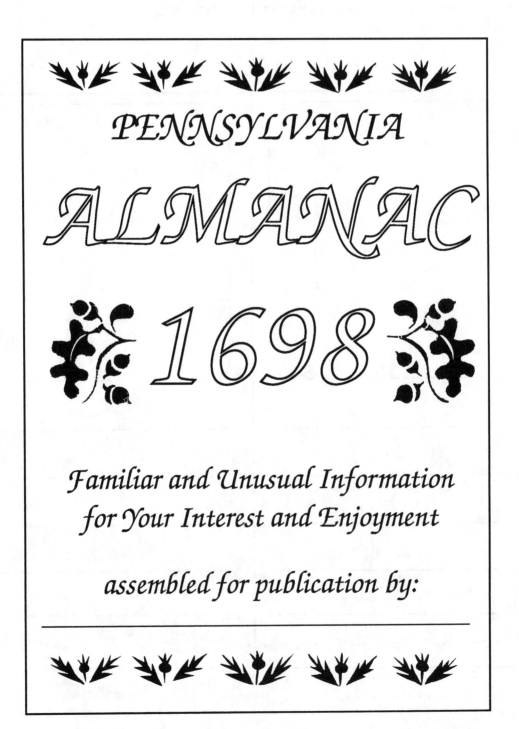

Colonial people referred to almanacs for necessary information. Be sure your facts are correct before you include them in your almanac pages!

Almanac Page

True and Official Knowledge About:

Pennsylvania Almanac 1698

Social Skills: Jog memory, probe by asking questions, seek accuracy.
Academic Skill: Understand how colonial children learned.
Teacher: Though tactics were sometimes negative, we think the children would enjoy re-creating this colorful schoolroom setting. Employ the co-op cards used to date, the almanacs and hornbooks or the *Schoolmaster Charade* game below to have the children re-create a traditional colonial classroom using information about school life from the introduction as a guide. Reproduce a set of *Colonial Quotations* on page 50.

SCHOOLMASTER GAME

The Interviewer is the schoolmaster and asks all the questions. Traditional schoolroom manners are required, along with discipline. Everyone should have a turn as schoolmaster.

Schoolmaster: Cut out the quotes.
Fold and put them in a box or hat
before you play this game.

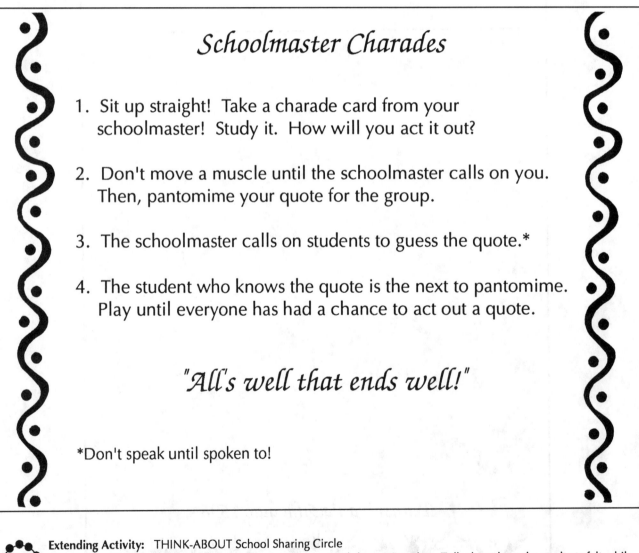

Schoolmaster Charades

1. Sit up straight! Take a charade card from your schoolmaster! Study it. How will you act it out?

2. Don't move a muscle until the schoolmaster calls on you. Then, pantomime your quote for the group.

3. The schoolmaster calls on students to guess the quote.*

4. The student who knows the quote is the next to pantomime. Play until everyone has had a chance to act out a quote.

"All's well that ends well!"

*Don't speak until spoken to!

Extending Activity: THINK-ABOUT School Sharing Circle
Compare and contrast how school was in colonial times with how it is today. Talk about how the students felt while playing the schoolmaster game.

Chapter 4: At Work

Teacher: This chapter contains information about how the colonists worked and how towns grew and prospered. It will be best to present the material step-by-step in this way: •Read Joseph Cavendish's letter to introduce the activity on pages 57 and 58. •Read Caleb Cavendish's letter to introduce pages 59-64. •Read Miles Cavendish's letter to introduce the activities on pages 68-70. •Complete the chapter with the sharing circle activity on the bottom of page 70.

June 14, 1703

Dear Caleb,

We are gladdened that you have opened your joiner shop in Philadelphia. You have a great talent for woodworking. The remodeling of our house is done. Now we have a parlor and kitchen on the first floor and three bedrooms upstairs. Your mother and Constance are always busy polishing and cleaning.

Our little farming community has grown into a small village. There is a meeting house and a one-room school. A schoolmaster will arrive after the crops are harvested. Our grist mill is doing a thriving business. We have traveling tinsmiths who come to repair our pots. Cobblers come to repair our shoes. Other farmers are providing services to us with barrel making and blacksmithing. Old Mr. Griffin has opened a general store in the front room of his house.

We have come a long way from our little one-room home with a few garden plots. America is a good place for us, as it will be for you. Take care in Philadelphia. We all miss you, but we know your future is in that busy seaport.

Your father,
Joseph Cavendish

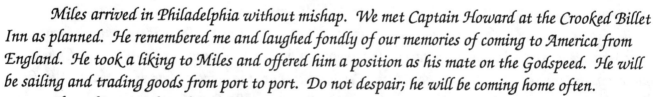

July 4, 1703

Dear Esteemed Parents,

Miles arrived in Philadelphia without mishap. We met Captain Howard at the Crooked Billet Inn as planned. He remembered me and laughed fondly of our memories of coming to America from England. He took a liking to Miles and offered him a position as his mate on the Godspeed. He will be sailing and trading goods from port to port. Do not despair; he will be coming home often.

How this town has changed since we arrived from England! It still has the orderly streets and houses with their little gardens. The pigs still roam the streets eating what garbage they can find in the gutters. The cows are still herded to the pasture each morning. But there are many more shops and street traders than when I was a child. Every sort of job imaginable is done here. Merchants and joiners like me sell wares from the front rooms of our houses. The kitchen and parlor are at the back and the bedrooms are above. I have a little garden planted in the rear yard. When Martha and I marry, we will be quite content here.

The streets are always busy with vendors. They go from door to door buying or selling all sorts of goods. Fish and poultry are sold. Old rags and tinware are collected to be made into new products. The streets are teeming with wagons of goods on their way to the wharf for shipping. Others deliver products to warehouses from the ships that sail in and out of port with every tide. Goods from all over the world arrive every day. There is a new beverage from China called tea. I am enclosing some for you to try. It is quite fashionable here.

Your humble son,
Caleb

September 6, 1703

Dear Esteemed Parents,

Since hiring on as a sailor with your old friend from the Godspeed, Captain Howard, I have traveled up and down the coast. Seeing the colonies has been an education. Today we docked at a plantation in Virginia. It is at least five hundred-fold bigger than our quaint farm in Pennsylvania. The main house sits above the river and the wharf. Huge hogshead barrels of tobacco were loaded aboard our vessel by black slaves. I do not approve of slavery. The poor souls will never be free. They are bought and sold like grain. Mr. Mauney, the plantation owner's son, told me that there are several hundred slaves at work on this vast plantation. He has never worked a day in his life, but he is expert enough in all the dealings of the plantation to know when a job is being done correctly. He has been following his father around since he was a toddler. That is how he learned the business.

The Mauney home is the finest mansion I have ever seen. It is built of brick made by slaves and has at least fourteen rooms, all elegantly furnished with the finest that can be imported from England and France. The huge dining room with carved furniture could seat fifty people. Hundreds of candles burn in crystal chandeliers. Behind the mansion is the kitchen. In the warm climate of Virginia wealthy landowners do not want to be bothered with the heat and smells from the kitchen. All the food is served on huge silver trays and in china tureens and carried to the house at mealtime by house slaves.

Located behind the kitchen and its gardens are the real workings of the plantation. There are buildings for every kind of work. Everything made in a small town can be manufactured here as well. Stables house all the horses and mules as well as the blacksmith. There is a weaving room where slaves make their blue linen garments. There is a building for every trade. Beyond all the work buildings are the tiny shanties of the slaves. Beyond those are the acres and acres of fields. All the food, flax and money crops like indigo or tobacco are grown on this huge farm.

During the evening the captain and I were invited to dine with the family. There were nine courses for dinner, each elegantly served by slave butlers. The family were all elegantly dressed in fine silks, brocades and lace. Even their shoes had silver buckles. There was much laughter and lots of music. The young mistress played delicate tunes for us on the harpsichord. She, like her brother, never has had to work. She is well versed in the running of a plantation house. Like her mother she will be head of a large home someday and will take care to the needs of all the slaves in the house and in the fields. She is the only doctor these people know. Learning how to set a broken bone and to use herbs and other plants for healing sickness are second nature to her.

I must close as we will soon be sailing with the tide. I hope that you all are well and have enjoyed the fine summer. You will be receiving more letters about my travels from every port.

Your roving son,
Miles

Social Skills: Work toward a goal, seek accuracy, no put-downs.
Academic Skill: Complete houses showing growth from small farms to villages.
Teacher: Team members each get sticker pieces to color and cut out. The *Farm to Village Scene* is passed around. Members place their *Stick-ems* where they fit best. Reproduce one set of *Stick-ems* and a *Farm to Village Scene* for each team.

FROM FARM TO VILLAGE

Work together to color and cut out the stick-em pieces. Pass the farm to village scene around for each member to add stick-ems to the scene.

Farm to Village Stick-ems

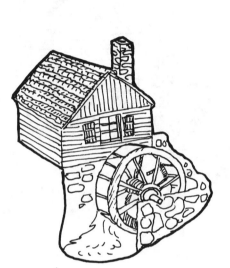

Farm to Village Scene

Extending Activity: DRAW-IT-DETAILS Simultaneous Activity
Four *Farm to Village Scenes* can be used without the *Stick-ems* for students to pass simultaneously, drawing in different details on each page.

Social Skills: Integrate ideas, elaborate, seek accuracy.

Academic Skills: Re-create an early city street scene.

Teacher: Reproduce one *Fold-Out* on tagboard for each member of the group. Note: The puppets on pages 36-39 can be reduced for use in the street scenes.

PHILADELPHIA FOLD-OUT

Teammates choose one strip to color and cut out. Assemble in any order you choose. Glue together end to end. Fold to stand. Add interesting details on tagboard such as people, animals and cobblestone streets. Fill shop windows with goods.

City Fold-Out

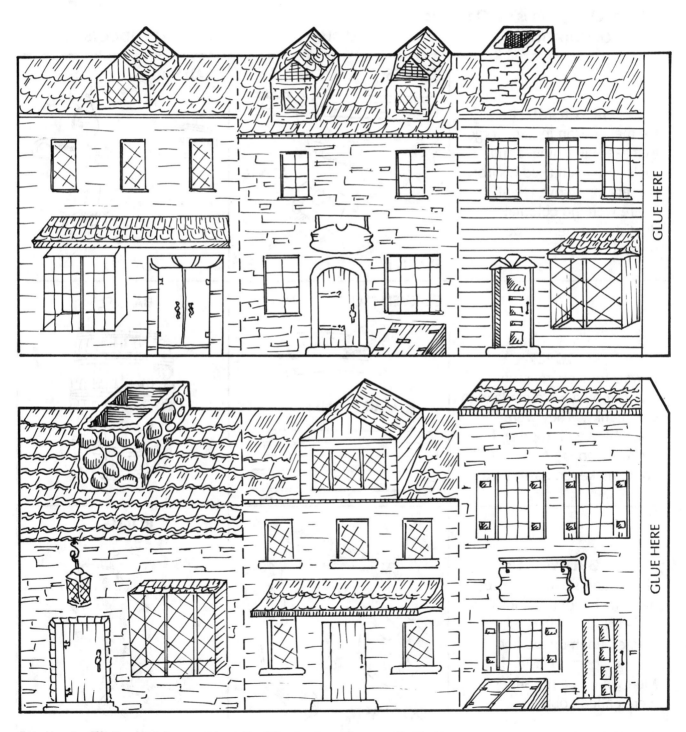

Social Skills: Form groups quietly, speak clearly, use quiet voices.
Academic Skill: Recognize and name goods and services related to various colonial occupations.
Teacher: Reproduce the *Colonial Occupation Co-op Cards* on pages 60-64 for this activity. Cut out. Give each student a card. Children with occupation/definition cards line up first and read their definitions out loud. Children with tools and products cards join them. **Note:** Use these cards with the *What's My Line?* game on page 66 and the *Bartering Game* on page 67.

COLONIAL OCCUPATIONS

If you have a definition card, line up first. Take turns reading cards aloud. If you have a tools or product card, decide what occupations your cards represent. Line up when it is read. When you are in your group, discuss the cards to learn the information.

Colonial Occupations Co-Op Cards

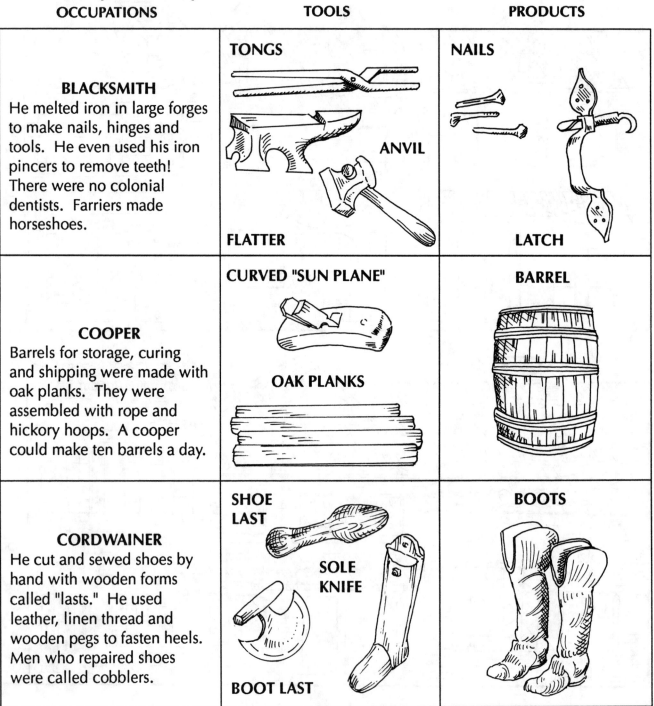

OCCUPATIONS	TOOLS	PRODUCTS
BLACKSMITH He melted iron in large forges to make nails, hinges and tools. He even used his iron pincers to remove teeth! There were no colonial dentists. Farriers made horseshoes.	TONGS / ANVIL / FLATTER	NAILS / LATCH
COOPER Barrels for storage, curing and shipping were made with oak planks. They were assembled with rope and hickory hoops. A cooper could make ten barrels a day.	CURVED "SUN PLANE" / OAK PLANKS	BARREL
CORDWAINER He cut and sewed shoes by hand with wooden forms called "lasts." He used leather, linen thread and wooden pegs to fasten heels. Men who repaired shoes were called cobblers.	SHOE LAST / SOLE KNIFE / BOOT LAST	BOOTS

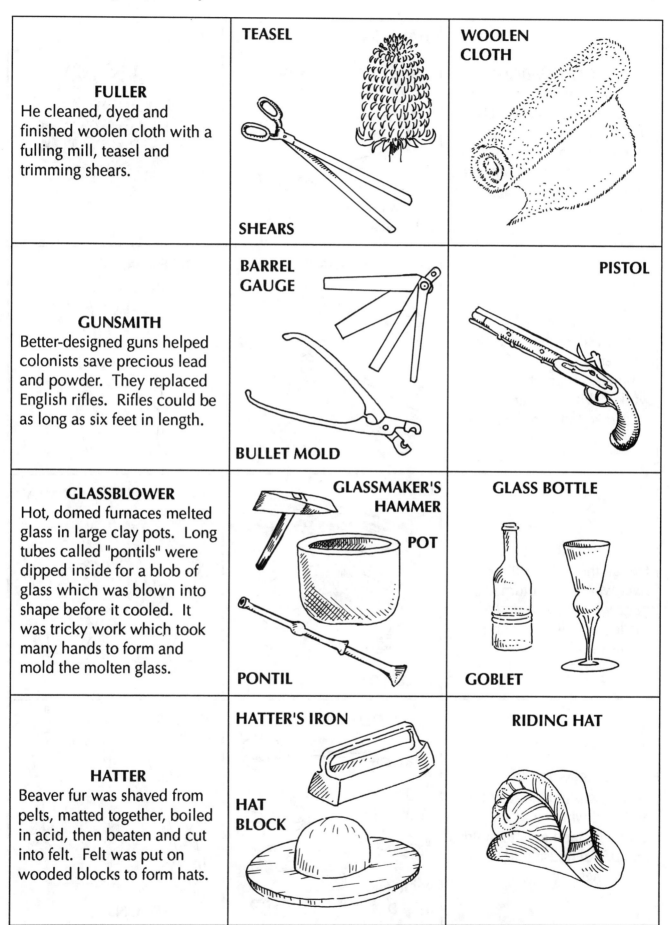

FULLER
He cleaned, dyed and finished woolen cloth with a fulling mill, teasel and trimming shears.

TEASEL

SHEARS

WOOLEN CLOTH

GUNSMITH
Better-designed guns helped colonists save precious lead and powder. They replaced English rifles. Rifles could be as long as six feet in length.

BARREL GAUGE

BULLET MOLD

PISTOL

GLASSBLOWER
Hot, domed furnaces melted glass in large clay pots. Long tubes called "pontils" were dipped inside for a blob of glass which was blown into shape before it cooled. It was tricky work which took many hands to form and mold the molten glass.

GLASSMAKER'S HAMMER

POT

PONTIL

GLASS BOTTLE

GOBLET

HATTER
Beaver fur was shaved from pelts, matted together, boiled in acid, then beaten and cut into felt. Felt was put on wooded blocks to form hats.

HATTER'S IRON

HAT BLOCK

RIDING HAT

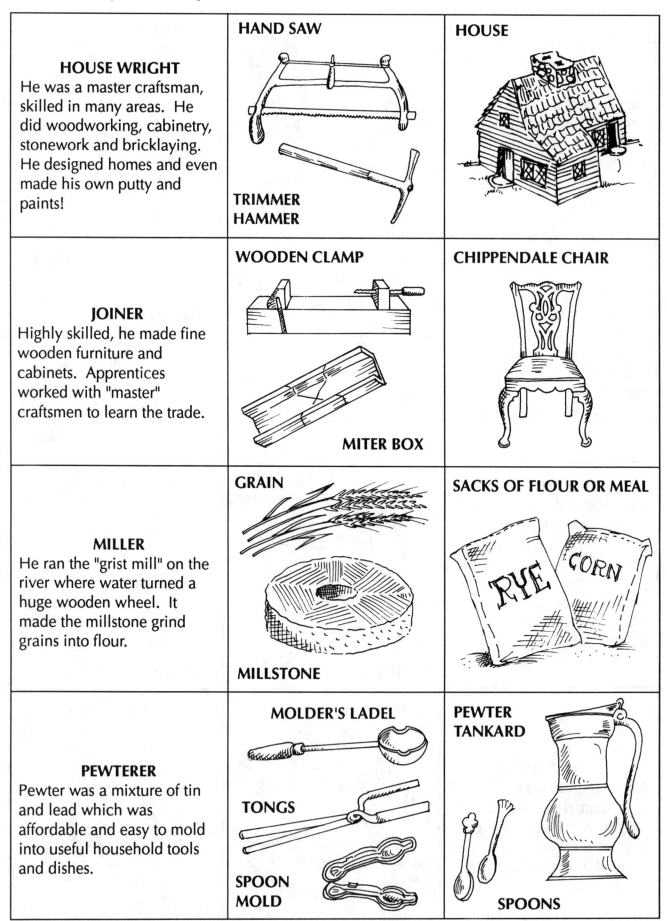

HAND SAW

HOUSE

HOUSE WRIGHT
He was a master craftsman, skilled in many areas. He did woodworking, cabinetry, stonework and bricklaying. He designed homes and even made his own putty and paints!

TRIMMER HAMMER

WOODEN CLAMP

CHIPPENDALE CHAIR

JOINER
Highly skilled, he made fine wooden furniture and cabinets. Apprentices worked with "master" craftsmen to learn the trade.

MITER BOX

GRAIN

SACKS OF FLOUR OR MEAL

MILLER
He ran the "grist mill" on the river where water turned a huge wooden wheel. It made the millstone grind grains into flour.

RYE CORN

MILLSTONE

MOLDER'S LADEL

PEWTER TANKARD

TONGS

PEWTERER
Pewter was a mixture of tin and lead which was affordable and easy to mold into useful household tools and dishes.

SPOON MOLD

SPOONS

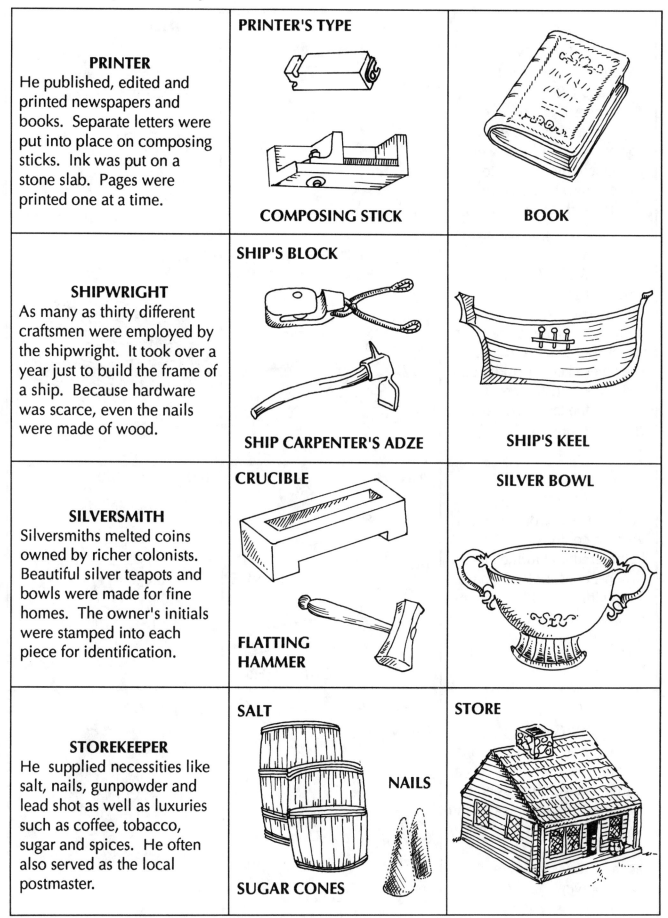

PRINTER
He published, edited and printed newspapers and books. Separate letters were put into place on composing sticks. Ink was put on a stone slab. Pages were printed one at a time.

PRINTER'S TYPE

COMPOSING STICK

BOOK

SHIPWRIGHT
As many as thirty different craftsmen were employed by the shipwright. It took over a year just to build the frame of a ship. Because hardware was scarce, even the nails were made of wood.

SHIP'S BLOCK

SHIP CARPENTER'S ADZE

SHIP'S KEEL

SILVERSMITH
Silversmiths melted coins owned by richer colonists. Beautiful silver teapots and bowls were made for fine homes. The owner's initials were stamped into each piece for identification.

CRUCIBLE

SILVER BOWL

FLATTING HAMMER

STOREKEEPER
He supplied necessities like salt, nails, gunpowder and lead shot as well as luxuries such as coffee, tobacco, sugar and spices. He often also served as the local postmaster.

SALT

STORE

NAILS

SUGAR CONES

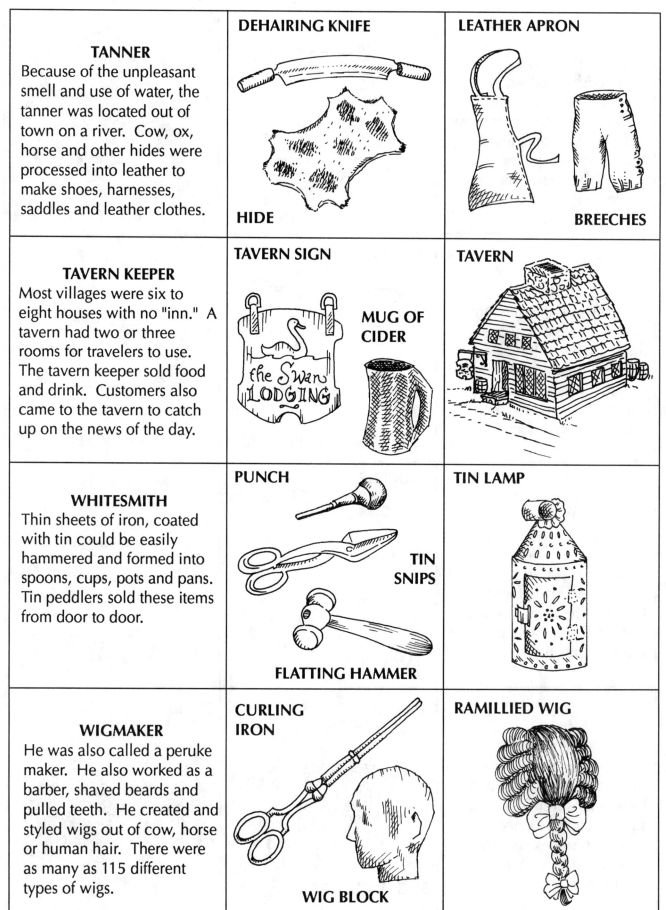

TANNER
Because of the unpleasant smell and use of water, the tanner was located out of town on a river. Cow, ox, horse and other hides were processed into leather to make shoes, harnesses, saddles and leather clothes.

DEHAIRING KNIFE

HIDE

LEATHER APRON

BREECHES

TAVERN KEEPER
Most villages were six to eight houses with no "inn." A tavern had two or three rooms for travelers to use. The tavern keeper sold food and drink. Customers also came to the tavern to catch up on the news of the day.

TAVERN SIGN

the Swan LODGING

MUG OF CIDER

TAVERN

WHITESMITH
Thin sheets of iron, coated with tin could be easily hammered and formed into spoons, cups, pots and pans. Tin peddlers sold these items from door to door.

PUNCH

TIN SNIPS

FLATTING HAMMER

TIN LAMP

WIGMAKER
He was also called a peruke maker. He also worked as a barber, shaved beards and pulled teeth. He created and styled wigs out of cow, horse or human hair. There were as many as 115 different types of wigs.

CURLING IRON

WIG BLOCK

RAMILLIED WIG

Social Skills: Plan carefully, speak clearly, work toward a goal.
Academic Skill: Work together to make descriptive sign.
Teacher: Reproduce *blank signs* and give one to each pair. Save to use in the *Bartering Game* on page 67.

SIGNS OF THE TIMES

Colonials hung clever signs outside their shops to illustrate their services. Design a sign with your partner for your business. Use the Colonial Occupations Co-op Cards to help you decide what to do.

Blank Signs

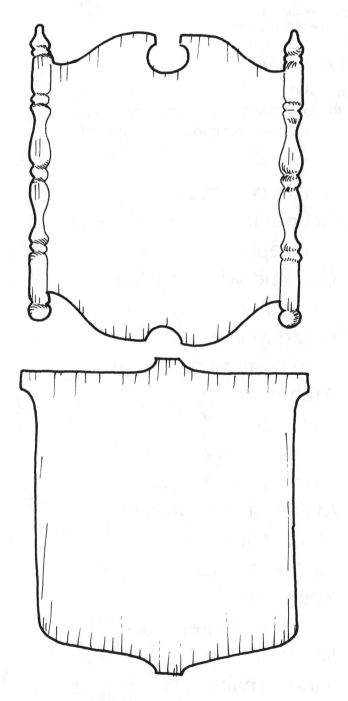

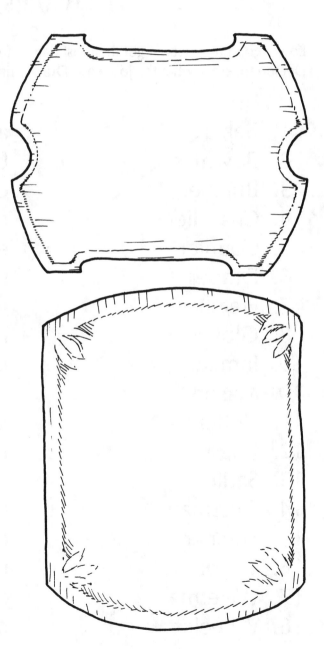

Extending Activity: Street Vendors' Street Cries
Street Vendors sold their wares from door to door. To get people's attention, they would sing ditties as they walked along. Example: "Hot cross buns! Hot cross buns! One a penny, two a penny. Hot cross buns!" Ask pairs to write a street cry for their business.

Social Skills: Speak clearly, listen actively, probe for answers.
Academic Skill: Recognize skills and services related to various colonial occupations.
Teacher: Keep the *Colonial Occupations Co-op Cards* on hand for this activity.

WHAT'S MY LINE?

Study groups assemble. Each member secretly chooses an occupation from the co-op cards. Take turns interviewing a member about his or her occupation. After each member has asked one question, each has a turn to guess what the occupation is. The one who gives the correct answer is the next member to be interviewed.

Social Skills: Speak clearly, listen actively, probe for answers.
Academic Skill: Recognize skills and services, deduce job from name.
Teacher: Reproduce one sheet for each pair.

WHAT'S IN A NAME?

guessing game

Long ago, many people got their last names from the jobs they did. Look over the names below. Decide together what the job was. Draw a line to the proper description. The first one is done for you.

1. Baker	a.	Maker of gloves
2. Bowman	b.	Accountant or bookkeeper
3. Butcher	c.	Innkeeper
4. Chandler	d.	Cart and wheel maker
5. Counter	e.	Nut seller
6. Draper	f.	Bread maker
7. Fletcher	g.	Ferryboat owner
8. Glover	h.	Archer
9. Inman	i.	Salt seller
10. Mason	j.	Candlemaker
11. Nutter	k.	Stonemason or cutter
12. Roper	l.	Maker of fine clothing
13. Sadler	m.	Meat seller
14. Saltzman	n.	Leather tanner
15. Skinner	o.	Rope maker
16. Taylor	p.	Arrow featherer
17. Waterman	q.	Seller of fabric
18. Wheeler	r.	Saddle maker

Answers: 1-f, 2-h, 3-m, 4-j, 5-b, 6-q, 7-p, 8-a, 9-c, 10-k, 11-e, 12-o, 13-r, 14-i, 15-n, 16-l, 17-g, 18-d.

Social Skills: Plan carefully, speak clearly, work toward a goal.
Academic Skill: Work together to make equitable trades.
Teacher: Reproduce a number of *Bartering Agreements* for each pair. Have all co-op cards and *Business Signs* from page 65 on hand. Pairs can also use crafts, foods and handiwork they have made for bartering.

BARTERING GAME

Colonists rarely had money to spend. They exchanged things they made or crops they grew for the things needed. That was called "bartering" or trading.

Pair up with your business partner. Put up your sign. Gather some crafts or copies of goods co-op cards to be "in business." One partner stays at the shop to be **Shopkeeper.** The other is the **Shopper** and goes to other businesses to barter their extra goods for other services, etc. Teams should plan carefully to make good trades!

Barter Agreement

Shopkeepers: Fill out one agreement for every customer.
Shoppers: Agree on what you will give in exchange for what you want, sign the agreement.

_____ *agrees to provide*
shopkeeper

_____

_____

in exchange for

_____

_____

signed: _____
customer

 Extending Activity: BARTERING Talk-About
Assemble as a class to discuss how you felt, what you accomplished during the bartering game.

Social Skills: Participate, work toward a goal, ask for help.
Academic Skill: Understand how a colonial plantation was organized.
Teacher: Reproduce one page of *Stick-ems* and a *Plantation Scene* for each group. Team members each get four *Stick-em* pieces to color and cut out. The *Plantation Scene* reproducible is passed around. Members place their stickers where they fit best. Keep the plantation activity on hand to use with comparison activities coming up.

BUILD-A-PLANTATION

Work together to color and cut out the stick-em pieces. Pass the Plantation Scene around for each member to add stick-ems where they fit in the scene.

Plantation Stick-ems

Social Skills: Speak clearly, listen actively, describe feelings.
Academic Skill: Understanding colonial life from different viewpoints.
Teacher: Reproduce an *Owner/Slave Comparison Chart* for each group.

PLANTATION LIFE

Family lives of plantation owners and slaves were very different. Think about what it was like to live on a plantation. Work together to fill in the sheet below. Compare the life of a plantation owner and a slave. How do you feel about each way of life?

Owner/Slave Comparison Chart

Plantation Owner's Family	Slave's Family
Homes:	
_____	_____
_____	_____
_____	_____
Family Life:	
_____	_____
_____	_____
_____	_____
Food:	
_____	_____
_____	_____
_____	_____
Clothes:	
_____	_____
_____	_____
Education:	
_____	_____
_____	_____
Social Life:	
_____	_____
_____	_____

Extending Activity: VILLAGE AND PLANTATION Talk-About
Look at the *Village and Plantation Stick-ems* assignments again. Discuss the likenesses and differences between them.

Extending Activity: PLANTATION LIFE Talk-About
Gather to discuss what pairs talked and wrote about.

Chapter 5: At Play

August 3, 1703

Dear Brother Miles,

You missed a lot of fun here yesterday. It was our summer Training Day. Several British officers in their bright red uniforms arrived. All the men from miles around were called to the village green to muster up. They marched all round and shot their rifles at targets. My husband, Harlan, really tried to look like a professional soldier. He will be expected to join all the other men if we are ever attacked. Training Day is just that: training!

While the men marched about to the drumbeats, all the children played all sorts of games. They pretended to march behind their brothers and fathers. Some went fishing in the pond. Others played Blind Man's Bluff. Some girls had a jump rope contest. Jacob even caught the greased pig!

Mother and I gossiped with the other married ladies. In the afternoon we had a great feast of all the food everyone had brought from home. We don't get many holidays, so everyone really played until sunset. Do you and your new wife, Martha, ever have fun in Philadelphia?

From your newly married sister to her just married brother,
Abigail

Social Skills: Work toward a goal, plan out loud, participate.
Academic Skills: Experience and re-create traditional colonial outdoor recreational activities.
Teacher: Study groups prepare a game for play, then number off to be ready to organize its play. Allow time for groups to prepare events.
On Training Day: Call out a number. The team member from each group with that number leads their team in setting up their event and stays on to be the first supervisor. The other teams members "PICK A SPOT" for other events. Set a time limit to switch "supervisors," so each member will have a turn to work and play. You will be free to supervise overall.

TRAINING DAY ACTIVITIES

GUNNY SACK RACES

Materials: Poster board and markers to make event signs. Four to six Large canvas or burlap sacks. Chalk, sand, small stones or boxes to mark start and finish lines for race.
Prepare to Play: Make the event signs. Decide how you will mark start and finish and get them ready. Make sure that players can fit inside the sacks, and that they come up to the waist. Team members should try "test-hopping" the race inside the sack to determine the best racing distance.
Play: Set up race markers. Place each bag along the starting line. A racer stands by each bag, and at the leader's signal slips the canvas sack over his or her feet and up to the waist. At the leader's signal, the racers hop inside the sacks to the finish line.

THREE-LEGGED RACE

Materials: Poster board and markers to make event signs. Three or four 1-yard lengths of fabric strips, soft rope or heavy cord. Chalk, sand, small stones or boxes to mark start and finish lines.
Prepare to play: Make the event signs. Mark start and finish and get them ready.
Play: Set up race markers. Line racers in 3-4 pairs side by side. The leader ties the players' inside legs together snugly right above the knee. Be sure not to tie it too tight! At the leader's signal the racers run together to the finish line.

FOOT RACE/OBSTACLE COURSE

Materials: Poster board and markers to make event signs and obstacle course diagram, chalk or rope to mark start and finish lines, natural materials such as rocks, bales of hay, burlap sacks, for obstacles.
Prepare to Play: Plan the "running course" for your playground. Agree on a plan and draw a diagram poster of it showing natural markers or other obstacles like rocks, sticks, bales of hay, sacks, etc. The poster will help the racers know where to go. Make sure you have all you need for the day of the race. Plan and make the markers and arrows to show the start, finish and turns to keep the runners going in the right direction.
Play: Set up the race markers and obstacle course. Racers line up along the finish line. On signal from the leader, racers run along the paths following the arrows to the finish line.

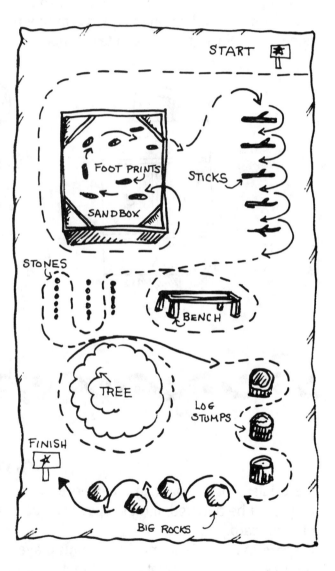

Teacher: Colonial men and boys enjoyed events testing their strength. This activity may be too physical for your students.

ARM WRESTLING

Materials: Poster board and markers to make event signs, 24" x 24" table or desk, two chairs, removable masking tape.

Prepare to Play: Make the event signs. To make the tabletop "wrestling arena," place tape down the middle of the table as shown. Place another line along either end to indicate areas in which contestants will place their elbows. Mark one side "A" the other side "B." Test the wrestling arena to make sure it's the right size for players to clasp hands when their elbows are in place. Adjust the tape on the table accordingly.

Play: Set up the event sign. Put the table and chairs on level ground. Two players will compete at a time. Contestants sit down, place their right elbows on the table and clasp hands firmly with their opponent. At the game leader's signal, players attempt to push their opponent's arm down onto the table. When one player's arm or wrist touches the table, the game is over. Winners can gain team points or have each team choose a representative to compete!

BOOT-PITCH

Materials: Poster board and markers to make event signs. Four old leather shoes or boots. If they can't be donated, thrift shops are a good resource for inexpensive boots. Two-foot squares of cardboard.

Prepare to Play: Determine the points players will earn for pitches and mark the cardboard with squares or rings for target areas. Practice pitching the boots at different distances to determine the best size "pitching field." Decide how many turns the players will get and how many points will win the game. Deduct points if the boot does not hit the target at all. Remember not to make the game play too long, so lots of players will be able to play.

Play: Place the pitching targets on opposite sides of the pitching field. One player stands near each square at each end of the pitching field. Players alternate tossing the boots onto the pitching targets and adding up points.

MUSTER AND MARCH

Materials: Poster board and markers to make event signs. Oatmeal box or coffee can with lid for drum. Brown paper, crayons and tape or glue to decorate drum.

Prepare to Play: To make a drum, cover the box or can with brown paper and decorate it for a "colonial" look. Make the event signs and markers. Create a special drum signal to indicate "line up." Compose another to indicate "march forward," "turn," "stop," etc. Beating regular beats sets the pace of the marching. Practice with your group to make sure everyone knows the signals and that they are simple to follow! Make event signs.

Play: Put up event signs in a large open area. Six to eight marchers will "muster up" at a time. The leader uses the drum to teach them the signals to line up and march. Practice to get everyone pacing together. Try other formations with faster or slower drumbeats.

 Teacher: This game can also be played in a straight line with ball being bounced against a wall. See what works best for your groups!

CALL BALL

Materials: Poster board and markers to make event signs, one 8-12" playground ball.

Prepare to Play: Make the event sign. Choose an area big enough for a circle of 6-8 children for your game.

Play: Six to eight players form a circle. Game leader is in the middle and starts play. Leader bounces the ball (hard!) on the ground. While it's in the air, the leader calls the name of a player who tries to catch the ball before it hits the ground. If successful, that player bounces next and calls another player's name.

BASKET BOWLING

Materials: Poster board and markers to make event signs, two softballs, bushel or wastebasket, string for "foul line" and "alleys."

Prepare to Play: You will need to decide how long to make the playing field and where the alleys will be. Generally, the longer the court and the narrower the alleys, the more skill needed to play. The target basket goes on its side at the end of the court between the "alleys." Determine what the points will be to hit the basket, go inside the basket, and what to deduct if you out of the "alley." Set up a test field and play it with the rules you've chosen to make sure the game is challenging, but still fun for all. Make an event sign and poster to explain the final rules.

Play: Put up the event/rule sign. Set the foul line, alley markers and basket in place on the playing field. On a signal from the leader, each player bowls the balls toward the basket.

STOOL BALL

Materials: Poster board and markers to make event signs, one soft playground ball, a short stool or closed cardboard carton, rope or tape to mark throwing line.

Prepare to Play: Put the stool or cardboard box in the playing area. Mark off the throwing line about 12 feet away from the stool. Practice playing the game. You may want to make the throwing line closer or farther away from the stool to make the game challenging, but fun. Make an event sign and poster listing your rules.

Play: One player, the "defender," stands by the stool. Three other players stand behind the throwing line. They take turns pitching the ball underhand, trying to hit the stool with the ball. The defender tries to bat the ball away before it hits the stool. Any player who hits the stool becomes the defender. Any player who catches the ball when it is batted back to the throwing line becomes the defender.

QUOITS

Materials: Poster board and markers to make event sign, three 18" pieces of stiff rope, duct tape, a 12" sturdy stick, tape or string to mark the tossing line.

Prepare to Play: Make three rings from rope and tape. Bend the rope into a circle with the ends overlapping about one inch. Tape securely. Slide the stick into the ground so that it is standing straight up. Practice trying to toss the rings onto the stick. You'll need to decide how far away from the stick players must stand to toss the rings. Decide on points for ringers and "leaners." Make an event sign and poster explaining your rules.

Play: Put up event/rule sign. Mark off your tossing line. Put the stick in the ground at the proper distance. Players take turns trying to ring the stick with the rope rings.

Social Skills: Stay in the group, work toward a goal, energize group.
Academic Skill: Experience and re-create traditional colonial recreational activities.
Teacher: In colonial times, gathering together was called a "bee." Colonists believed it was easier to do anything in a group than individually, so bees were used for many purposes. Try some of these with your groups to have them discover the fun of working together to accomplish a common goal.

ALL KINDS OF BEES

Teacher: Read the instructions carefully to see how we changed the rules for a cooperative classroom activity! Reproduce a *Spelling Bee List* for each group. Gather lists to make a master list to distribute to all the groups.

COOPERATIVE SPELLING BEE

Materials: Each team prepares a list of 10-20 spelling words by pulling names from co-op cards or other colonial resources.

Prepare to Play: Practice all the spelling bee words. Pair up and create co-op cards or round-robin the spelling words. Number off in your group for play.

Play: The teacher or leader calls a number. Team members with that number stand. Each takes a turn spelling a word from the list. If a player misses a word, he or she may not stand again. The team with the most members still standing gets credit for being the best-prepared!

Spelling Bee List

Spelling Bee Word List Group:———			

Teacher: If children are too young to use a potato peeler, don't do this event! Potatoes can also be used, but we think that apples have tastier possibilities! Depending on the ages of your students, their skill level, and the total number of apples to peel, set a given time limit for peeling. Cheer them on as they work, praising the neatest workers, etc. Use the "apple" award for the last group to finish or the first group to find a wormy apple!
Extending Activity: Use the peeled apples to make dried apples (page 30), apple head dolls (page 86), or applesauce (page 31). **Note:** Cut apples should be used right away. Plan ahead for follow-up activities and allow enough time to do both! If you will be delayed, sprinkle apples with lemon to keep browning to a minimum!

APPLE PEELING BEE

Materials: Each child brings in a few apples, a potato peeler, a few newspapers and a brown bag from home. Each group will need a clean bowl to collect peeled apples.
Prepare to Play: Wash apples and hands. Spread newspapers on desk and roll top of brown bag down to collect apple peelings.
Play: Peel apples. Put the peelings in the brown bag and peeled apples in the bowl. How long a peel can you keep in one piece?

Apple Peeling Bee Award

Apple Award to:

Teacher: Talk to a local farmer to determine the best corn to use for this activity and when it could be affordably available. The farmer can also suggest other uses for the type of corn you will be husking. Perhaps you can give it back to the farm for animal feed or plan a classroom corn roast.
Extending Activity: Use the corn husks to make dolls (page 88). Dried or colored ornamental corn can be used to make harvest decorations.

COOPERATIVE CORNHUSKING BEE

Materials: Two or three ears of corn per member, 1 brown bag per member, a large tub or bucket to hold finished corn.
Prepare to Play: Place classroom chairs in a big circle or two smaller circles. Place 2-3 ears of corn under each chair. Place a brown paper bag in front of each chair. The large bucket goes in the center of the circle.
Play: At a given signal, each child takes an ear of corn from under his or her chair and pulls one husk off, then passes it on. When the cob is clean, that child places it in the center bucket and starts another one. Keep on husking and passing until all the corn is done. This is a good activity to encourage friendly conversation or singing together. You'll all be surprised how fast a big job gets done!

Teacher: Give a *Cleaning Bee Role Card* to each group. Children bring in appropriate cleaning materials on cleaning day. It's best to give a time limit. When done, praise them for making their classroom sparkle! Plan an extending activity to reward them for their industry!

CLASSROOM CLEANING BEE

Prepare to Play: Depending on your group's role, plan how you will organize to do the job on cleaning day. You may want to split up in pairs, or each take one section of the room. For instance, the broom/dustpans teams could split up the room or help each other move desks while the other sweeps. Write down your plan and get your teacher's approval.

Play: Dress in work clothes on cleaning day. At a given signal gather your materials and do your job as your group planned it.

Cleaning Bee Role Cards:

Dust Busters	*Dirt Dabbers*
Materials: dust cloths Dust classroom shelves and bookcases.	**Materials:** soapy water and rags Wash down desks and counter tops.
Clean Sweepers	*Squeaky Cleaners*
Materials: brooms and dustpans Sweep out classroom and closets.	**Materials:** window cleaner and rags Clean mirrors, sinks and lower inside windows.

Teacher: Students bring their quilting square from page 44 to make into a larger quilt piece. You may want to combine study groups together to make an even larger quilt.

QUILTING BEE

Materials: One 12" x 12" square of butcher paper, glue, Four 6" quilt squares
Prepare to Play: Lay out the squares on the butcher paper in an arrangement you all like.
Play: Pass the butcher paper around the group as you each glue a square in place.

COLONIAL SONGS AND RHYMES

Social Skills: Summarize, paraphrase, speak clearly.
Academic Skill: Learn and share traditional colonial rhymes, songs and chants.
Teacher: Students learn colonial songs, chants and rhymes together. A few are shown here to get you started. Children can make up body motions, dances or rope-skipping patterns to perform for the rest of the class.
Extending Activity: STAND AND SHARE songs with other partners.

 SING-A-SONG OR SAY-A-RHYME

Pick a rhyme or tune to learn with your partner. Plan body movements, rope-skipping pattern or dance to perform for the class.

The Muffin Man

Oh, do you know the muffin man, the muffin man, the muffin man
Oh, do you know the muffin man that lives in Drury Lane! Oh!

Oh, yes we've seen the muffin man, the muffin man, the muffin man
Oh, yes we've seen the muffin man that lives in Drury Lane! Oh!

Yankee Doodle

Yankee Doodle went to town a-riding on a pony
He stuck a feather in his hat and called it macaroni.
Yankee Doodle keep it up, Yankee Doodle Dandy
Mind the music and the step and with the girls be handy.

The Old Gray Goose

Go tell Aunt Rhody, go tell Aunt Rhody,
Go tell Aunt Rhody the old gray goose is dead.

The one she's been savin', the one she's been savin'
The one she's been savin' to make a feather bed.

She drowned in the millpond, she drowned in the millpond,
She drowned in the millpond standing on her head.

Old gander's weepin', old gander's weepin',
Old gander's weepin', because his wife is dead.

The goslins are mournin', goslins are mournin',
Goslins are mournin', 'cause their mammy's dead

She only had one feather, she only had one feather,
She only had one feather, a-stickin' in her head.

Hot Cross Buns

Hot cross buns! Hot cross buns!
One a-penny, two a-penny, hot cross buns!

If you have no daughters, if you have no daughters,
If you have no daughters, then give them to your sons.

But if you have none of these little elves
You must eat them all yourselves.

Little Boy Blue

Little Boy Blue, come blow your horn
The sheep's in the meadow,
The cow's in the corn.
Where is the boy who looks after the sheep?
He's under the haystack, fast asleep!

Counting Rhyme

Note: This rhyme helped colonial children
        learn and remember their chores:

One, two, buckle my shoe

   (get up early in the morning)

Three, four, shut the door

   (shut cottage door to keep out farm animals)

Five, six, pick up sticks

   (gather wood for kindling and fire)

Seven, eight, lay them straight

   (stack them up near the fireplace)

Nine, ten, a big fat hen.

   (gather eggs from the hen house)

Eleven, twelve, dig and delve.

   (help in the garden)

Social Skills: Integrate ideas into one, work toward a goal, ask for help when needed.
Academic Skill: Plan and make improvised colonial musical instruments.
Teacher: Pairs create simple handmade instruments, then take turns plucking or humming along to accompany each other as they do the rhymes and songs from the previous activity.

MUSIC MAKERS TO TAP, HUM AND STRUM

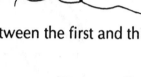

MUSICAL SPOONS

Materials: Two metal spoons per player.
To Play: Rest the spoon bowl bottoms together, holding the handles between the first and third fingers. Tap the spoons against your hand or leg to play.

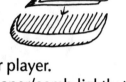

COMB AND PAPER HUM-DINGER

Materials: One pocket-size comb and small piece of thin tissue paper per player.
To Play: Fold the paper and slide over the teeth of the comb. Hold the paper/comb lightly to your lips as you hum or breath lightly against the side of the comb. Practice blowing and holding the comb to make it sound like a kazoo.

JUG AND BOTTLE BAND

Materials: Small cola bottles, a variety of sizes of jugs.
To Play: Fill bottles with different amounts of water, blow across the tops to see what sounds they make. Adjust lips, angle of jug and blowing to get the best sound. Arrange the bottles by pitch and try to create songs by blowing the different bottles.

TWIG STRUMMER

Materials: Y-Shaped twig, a number of thin rubber bands for each instrument.
To Play: Stretch the bands at different places across the twig. Make sure they are rather tight. Pluck them and adjust tightness to make each band sound differently.

COLONIAL GAMES GALORE

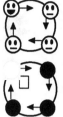

Social Skill: Integrate a number of ideas, work together toward a goal, check answers.
Academic Skill: Remember and record complete directions for traditional games.
Teacher: Groups work out step-by-step directions together using the role cards of RECORDER, CHECKER, GATEKEEPER and QUIET CAPTAIN from the appendix. **Note:** Have them round-robin their ideas orally before writing them to make sure all agree. Give the class time to share and play these familiar games.

TELL-A-GAME

Pick a game familiar to your group. Choose from: Blind Man's Bluff, Hopscotch, Hide and Seek, London Bridge or Tag. Round-robin the steps to play. Write out the directions.

Social Skills: Use quiet voices, generate further answers, work together toward a goal.
Academic Skill: Create different designs and record them.
Teacher: Reproduce one *Tangram Puzzle* for each pair to cut out. After the activity, put *Tangram Puzzle* outlines in a special classroom display for use during free time.

MAKE-A-GAME

Cut out the puzzle pieces and work with your partner to rearrange the pieces in various ways to make pictures or objects. For each puzzle solution you make, draw an outline of it to keep and exchange. Do three or four puzzles.

Tangram Puzzle Pieces

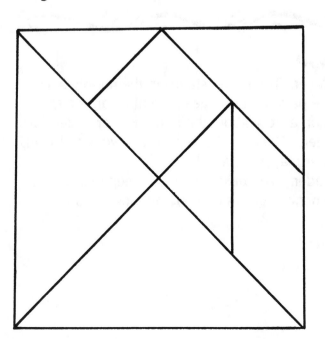

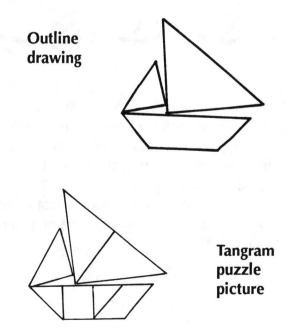

Outline drawing

Tangram puzzle picture

Social Skills: Speak clearly, generate further answers, listen carefully.
Academic Skill: Developing fluent thinking and memory skills.
Teacher: Assign a leader for the games or start them yourself. Be sure everyone knows which direction play will move around the circle.

LARGE GROUP GAMES

COOPERATIVE TWENTY QUESTIONS

To Play: The leader thinks of a name of any colonial object. Starting where the leader chooses, each player around the circle in turn asks a question about it. Up to 20 questions can be asked. Players can guess at any time, but only the one that guesses correctly will be the next leader. If no one has guessed correctly by the end of the questioning, the leader chooses his or her successor, who picks a new word and starts play again.

COOPERATIVE BEAST, BIRD OR FISH

To Play: The leader sits in the middle of a circle. The leader points to someone in the circle and names a category...BEAST, BIRD OR FISH. Starting with that person, everyone take turns naming an object in that category around the circle until the leader counts to ten. The last person to name the object becomes the next leader. Be sure to keep your eyes and ears open, as this is a fast-paced game!

HUNTSMAN

To Play: Move chairs into a circle, one for every player. The leader stands in the middle and gives everyone in the circle a name of things that are part of a hunt; gear, clothing, animals, etc. Then the leader walks around in the circle, making up a story about the hunt. Players listen for their object to be named, then walk behind the leader. When the hunter has everyone following him, he sits down quickly and says "bang!" The other players scramble for a seat. Whoever is left out because the leader took a seat is the next leader. The next leader can keep the same names and tell a new story or give new names in other categories (farmer supplies, ocean voyage tales).

Social Skills: Use names, make eye contact, participate.
Academic Skill: Plan and make colonial toys.
Teacher: These toys are so simple and fun; each partner will want to make one! Each pair gets the directions and plans together to make one toy.

COLONIAL TOYS

Partners: Make a list of all the materials you will need to make a toy. Divide up the list and be responsible for bringing items from home. Can you design other colonial toys together?

BUZZ SAW

Materials: Two 3" sticks, 20" string, 1" (or larger) button.
To Make: Fold the string in half and tie the folded end to one stick. Thread string through holes in the button. Move the button to the center. Tie the ends of the string to the other stick.
To Play: Hold a stick in each hand and let the button hang down. Flip it to wind the string around and around. When the string is twisted, pull outward on the sticks to get the button spinning and sounding like a "buzz saw." Keep pulling and relaxing the string to keep the button going. Challenge your partner to keep it going longer!

BUTTON AND CUP

Materials: Straight, sturdy 8" stick or unsharpened pencil, egg carton cup, 1" button, 20" length of string.
To Make: Poke the stick carefully through the bottom of the egg carton cup so it sits 1/2" from end. Tie the string to the end of the stick. Tie the button to the end of the string.
To Play: Hold the cup end out in front of you and move the stick to flip the button on the string into the cup. Count how many times you are successful within a time limit or number of attempts. The string can be made longer to make it harder or shorter to make it easier to play.

BUTTON BOLO

Materials: 20" length of string, two identical, heavy buttons, 1" or bigger.
To Make: Tie a button to each end of the string.
To Play: Try to make the buttons orbit in opposite directions by holding the string in the center and moving your hand up and down. It takes practice!

Social Skills: Use names, make eye contact, participate.
Academic Skill: Plan and make colonial dolls out of natural materials.
Teacher: Use the the apples from the *Apple Peeling Bee* on page 78 for the dolls. Use the corn husks from the *Cornhusking Bee* on page 78.

COLONIAL DOLLS

Teacher: Allow time for the project: Heads: 20 minutes preparation, 7-10 days drying. Head finishing: 20 minutes. Bodies: 30-40 minutes to cut out and paste clothing on dolls. Be prepared to help if coat hanger is hard to bend!

APPLE HEAD DOLLS

Work together to make one doll. Take turns following each step.

Materials For Head: Plastic knife, 1 firm peeled apple, two cloves, four white peppercorns, lightweight metal hanger, lacquer, red or pink marker, glue, yarn or fake fur for hair

To Make Head:

1. Carve small hollows in the apple for eyes. Push a clove in each hollow for eyeballs.
2. Cut along cheek area to carve nose.
3. Cut a slit under the nose for the mouth. Push peppercorns into the mouth slit for teeth.
4. When the face is done, take a hanger and straighten the hooked top.   Slide it directly through the center of the apple. This will be the wire base for your body.
5. Re-curve the hanger top, label it and hang it in an airy place. Each day, gently press features into shape.
6. After 7-10 days, spray or paint a coat of lacquer over the dried apple. Let dry.
7. Color the cheeks and lips with a marker. Glue on bits of yarn or fake fur for hair.

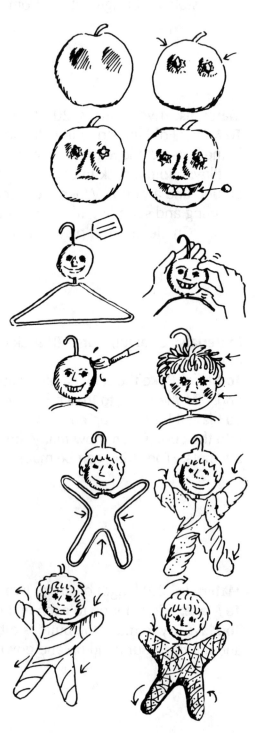

Materials for Body: 6-8 paper towels, 4-6 12" strips masking tape, felt for hands, shoes, 12" x 12" calico/gingham prints cut in 1 1/2" strips, scissors, tacky glue

To Make Body:

1. Bend the hanger to make arms and legs as shown.
2. Pad the hanger with one or two layers of paper towels.
3. Wrap the padded hanger tightly with masking tape to secure.
4. Wrap fabric strips around doll to cover tape. Glue ends.
5. Cut out patterns from page 87. Trace on felt. Cut out.
6. Glue hands to the ends of the arms. Glue boots to ends of legs.
7. Hang from hanger ends or trim hanger with wire snips.

86

Apple Head Doll Patterns

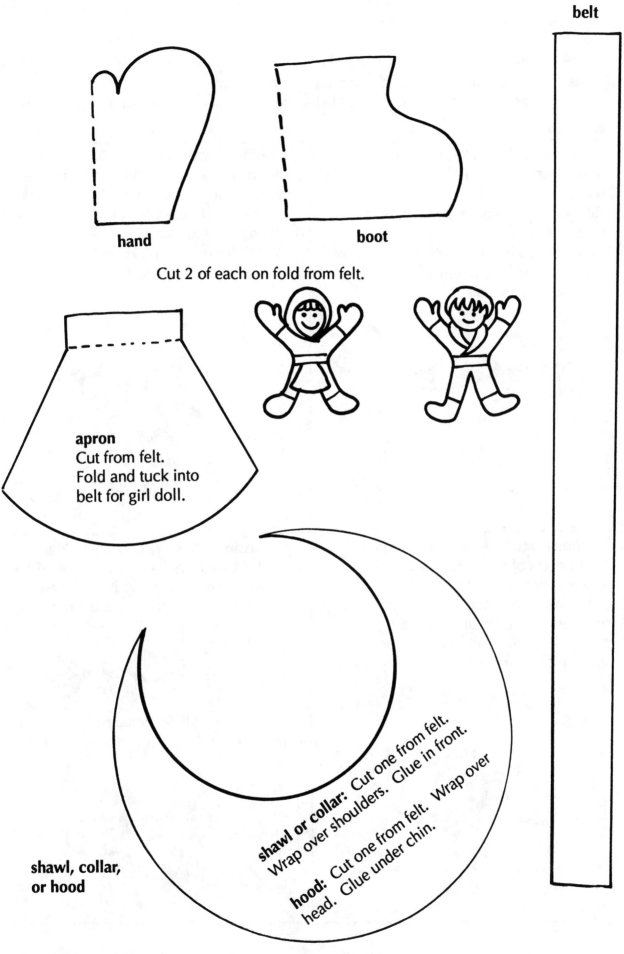

belt

hand

boot

Cut 2 of each on fold from felt.

apron
Cut from felt.
Fold and tuck into
belt for girl doll.

shawl or collar: Cut one from felt.
Wrap over shoulders. Glue in front.

hood: Cut one from felt. Wrap over
head. Glue under chin.

**shawl, collar,
or hood**

Teacher: Using the role cards as a guide, team members create dolls in a round table fashion, then decorate their own. Use the corn husks from the *Cornhusking Bee* on page 78 for the dolls. **Note:** Cold water dyes or vegetable dyes can be add to the soaking water to color the husks.

CORN HUSK DOLLS

Materials: dried cornshucks, pieces of cotton, thin string, corn silk or yarn.

Note: Shucks should be soaked 30 minutes before making dolls. Keep them damp while using.

Teammate 1: Makes Dolls' Heads

1. Make 4 heads. Form 4 cotton wads into 4 balls.
2. Take shucks and place a cotton wad in the center of each one.
3. Tie string around the shuck at the base of the cotton ball to from head.
4. **Pass on to Teammate 2.**

Teammate 2: Makes Dolls' Arms

1. Make 4 sets of arms. Take several husks and roll them into tubes.
2. Tie string at each end to make wrists.
3. Slip between husks under head.
4. Stuff with cotton and tie below for waist.
5. **Pass on to Teammate 3.**

Teammate 3: Makes Dolls' Legs

1. Make 4 sets of legs. Split each main shuck lengthwise up the middle 1/2" from waist.
2. Add more shucks. Tuck them in the waist.
3. Tie again at the waist.
4. Tie off leg ends to make feet.
5. **Pass on to Teammate 4.**

Teammate 4: Makes Dolls' Hair

1. Make 4 heads of hair. Glue or tie corn silk or yarn to head, making it in various styles.
2. **Pass one doll back to each teammate.**

All Teammates:

Add faces and clothing details to your doll.

Chapter 6: Colony Maps and Facts

March 12, 1715

Dear Honorable Parents,

I am writing to you from Boston in the Massachusetts Bay Colony to let you know I have been promoted to captain on the Endeavor. She is a fine ship, a three-master. She will continue to lade cargo to and from the Indies and the colonies under my command.

As you know, in my years at sea I have visited all thirteen colonies. I have come to think of them as thirteen pieces to the same puzzle. Each one is different in many ways. All thirteen have surveyed their land and discovered its assets. All are raising crops and mining natural resources that are profitable for export to England or other colonies. But they are alike in more ways. All are working to make a living in America. All are under English rule and must answer to a king who is all the way across the Atlantic Ocean.

Here, on this side of the Atlantic, I have met people from many lands in Europe. All are bringing their special customs and talents to make new lives for themselves, just like you did twenty-five years ago. There are Scotch Irish, French Huguenots, Germans, Swedes, Dutch, almost every country in Europe. I heard someone say the other day that the colonies are like a huge melting pot of many peoples. Do you have any idea what he meant by that?

Your loving son,
Miles

 Social Skills: Form groups quietly, probe for answers, listen actively.
Academic Skill: Use map and reading skills with colonial maps.
Teacher: Reproduce a *Map Facts and Find-Its* sheets for each team from pages 90-93. Set up an area of the classroom for each colony section. Children go to the area of their choice. Pair them up to use materials.

MAP FACTS AND FIND-ITS
Cut apart the Find-Its Cards and place them face down between you. Take turns picking a card, reading it and finding the answers on the map.

Extending Activity: MAP FACTS SWITCH
Another day students choose a different colony section and partner to play Find-Its again. They may want to make up questions of their own.

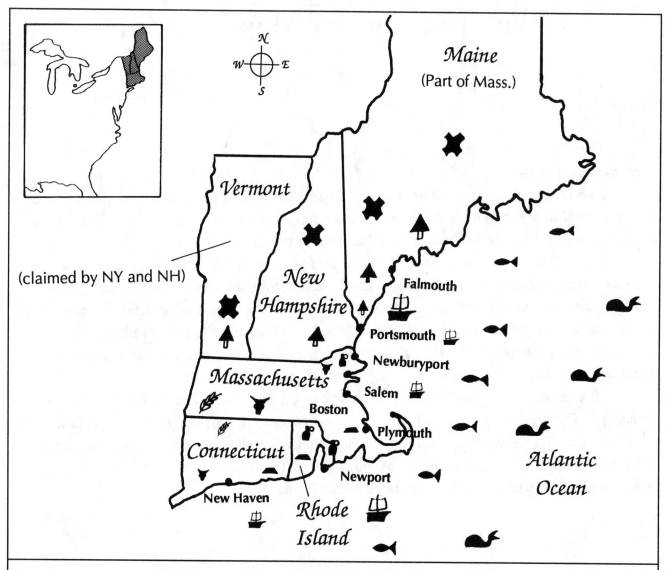

New England Map and Fact Sheet

Colony (Year Founded)	Founding Leader	Reasons for Founding

Massachusetts
    Plymouth (1620)
    Massachusetts Bay (1630)
	William Bradford
	John Winthrop
		Religious freedom
		Religious freedom

New Hampshire (1622)	Ferdinando Gorges John Mason	Profit from fishing and fur trade

Connecticut
    Hartford (1636)
    New Haven (1639)
	Thomas Hooker	Expand trade, religious and political freedom

Rhode Island (1636)	Roger Williams	Religious freedom

Chief Products

cattle　　fish　　furs　　grain　　iron　　lumber　　rum　　ships　　whales

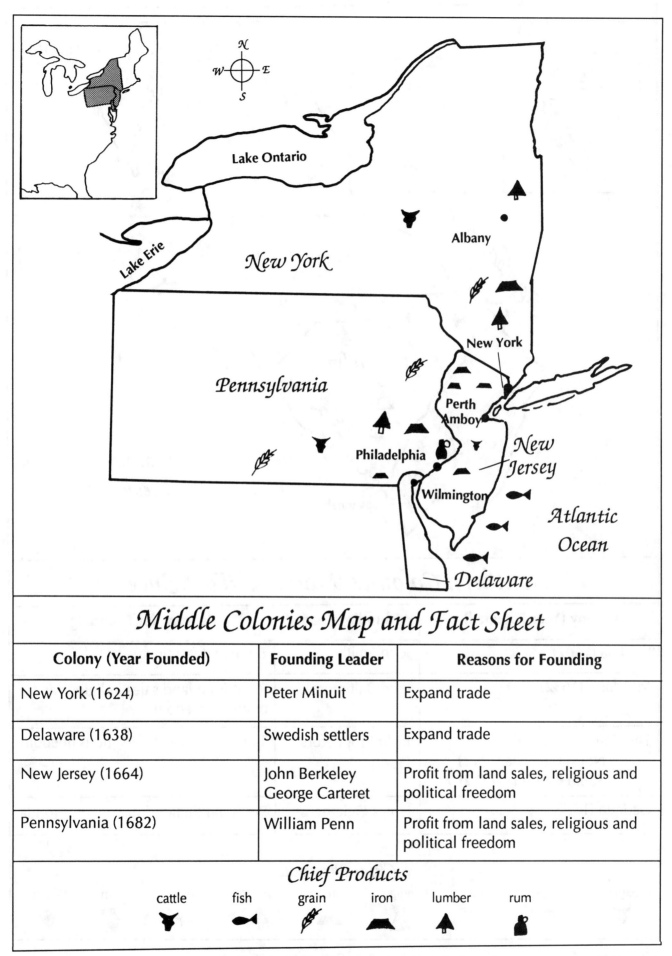

Middle Colonies Map and Fact Sheet

Colony (Year Founded)	Founding Leader	Reasons for Founding
New York (1624)	Peter Minuit	Expand trade
Delaware (1638)	Swedish settlers	Expand trade
New Jersey (1664)	John Berkeley George Carteret	Profit from land sales, religious and political freedom
Pennsylvania (1682)	William Penn	Profit from land sales, religious and political freedom

Chief Products

cattle   fish   grain   iron   lumber   rum

Use with *Find-Its Quiz Cards* on page 93 and *Post Rider Game* on pages 95 and 96.

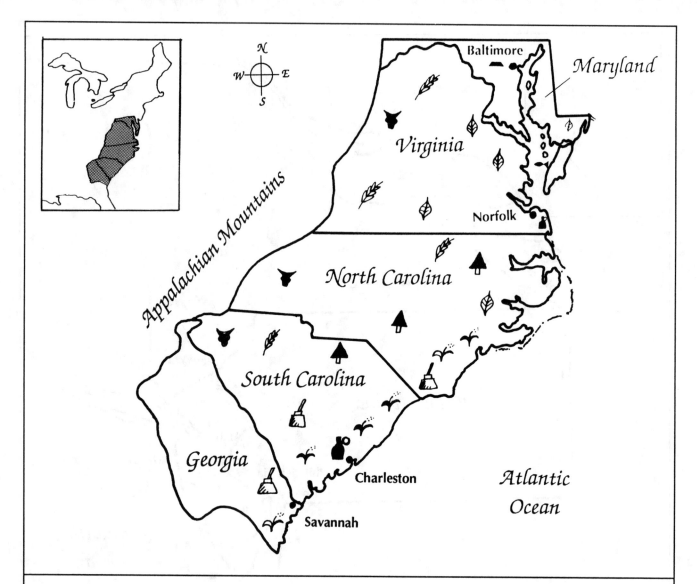

Southern Colonies Map and Fact Sheet

Colony (Year Founded)	Founding Leader	Reasons for Founding
Virginia (1607)	John Smith	Trade and farming
Maryland (1632)	Lord Baltimore	Profit from land sales, religious and political freedom

The Carolinas (1663)
    North Carolina (1712)
    South Carolina (1712)
	Eight Proprietors	Trade and farming, religious freedom

Georgia (1732)	James Oglethorpe	Profit, protection from enemy Florida

Chief Products

cattle	fish	grain	indigo	iron	lumber	rice	rum	tobacco

Number 1 Partner 1. Name a colony. Partner 2. Name a city there.	**Number 9** Partner 1. Name a seaport. Partner 2. Name another seaport.
Number 2 Partner 1. Name a product. Partner 2. Name colonies that made that product.	**Number 10** Partner 1. Are the products mostly natural or manufactured? Partner 2. Name them.
Number 3 Partner 1. Which colony was most productive? Partner 2. Name other colonies that made those products.	**Number 11** Partner 1. Which colonies were founded before 1630? Partner 2. Name those founded after 1630.
Number 4 Partner 1. Pick a colony. Name a colony that is north or south of it. Partner 2. Guess the colony your partner chose.	**Number 12** Partner 1. Which colony had more than one founder? Partner 2. Name another founder.
Number 5 Partner 1. What was the most-produced product in these colonies? Partner 2. Find the least-produced product.	**Number 13** Partner 1. Name three products. Partner 2. Find a colony that made all three.
Number 6 Partner 1. Which colony was founded for religious freedom? Partner 2. Name another.	**Number 14** Partner 1. Name a year a colony was founded. Partner 2. Find and name the colony.
Number 7 Partner 1. Which colony was founded to extend trade? Partner 2. Name another.	**Number 15** Partner 1. Which colony is farthest north? Partner 2. Which colony is farthest south?
Number 8 Partner 1. Which is the smallest colony shown? Partner 2. Name the largest colony shown.	**Number 16** Partner 1. Which colony is farthest east? Partner 2. Which colony is farthest west?

Social Skills: Seek accuracy, work toward a goal, integrate ideas.
Academic Skill: Recognize and identify colony shapes and put them in order on a map.
Teacher: Reproduce a set of *Mix-a-Map Shapes* for each group.

MIX-A-MAP

Divide the shapes to color and cut out in your group. Guess each colony by its shape. Label them. Fit the shapes together to make a map of each colony section.

Mix-a-Map Shapes

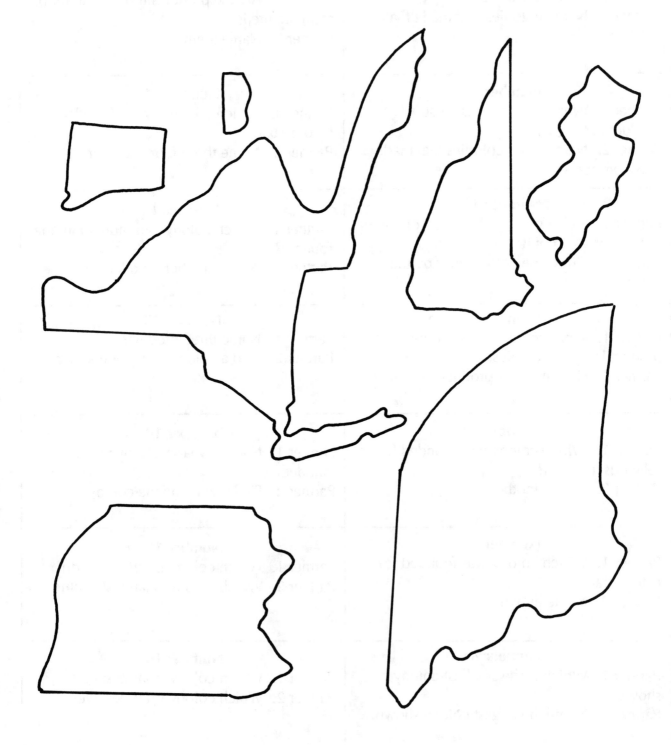

Mix-a-Map Shapes

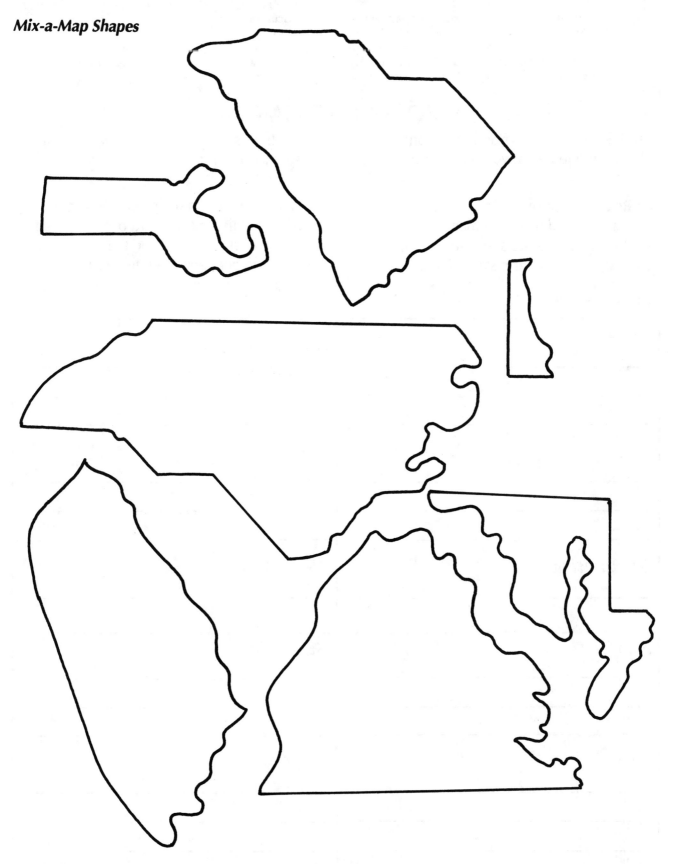

Social Skills: Participate, plan out loud, integrate a number of ideas.
Academic Skill: Apply information found in one source to another.
Teacher: Display the *Map/Fact Sheets* or have other resources available to complete atlas pages.
Extending Activity: CLASSROOM ATLAS
Each group designs a full page for each colony using the Mix-a-Map shape as a guide. Research additional information such as land formations in the area, nationalities in each colony and rivers. Bring them together into a classroom atlas.

Social Skills: Integrate ideas, participate, generate further discussion.
Academic Skill: Recognize cities and points of interest across maps.
Teacher: Reproduce a set of *Trip Starter Cards* below and one *Post Rider Bag* per group. Give them a *Map/Fact Sheet* (page 87) for an area of their choice. To play the game, put a map on an overhead projector, use your own colony map or enlarge a *Map/Fact Sheet* for use in front of the class.

POST RIDER GAME

Post riders carried news and mail from colony to colony. In this game your group will tour the colonies and tell what you see as you travel from one spot to another.

Get Ready: Each member of the group fills out a trip starter card using the map. Work together to color, cut out, paste and assemble the post rider bag. Tuck your trip starter cards inside.

Play: Number off in the group. When your number is called, pull a card out of the bag. Show the post rider route on the large map. For an extra challenge, put two or more cards together for a longer trip.

Trip Starter Cards

Start:	*Start:*
_____	_____
_____	_____
See:	*See:*
_____	_____
_____	_____
Destination:	*Destination:*
_____	_____
Start:	*Start:*
_____	_____
_____	_____
See:	*See:*
_____	_____
_____	_____
Destination:	*Destination:*
_____	_____

Post Rider Bag Pattern

Use with the *Trip Starter Cards* on page 96.

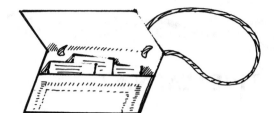

Post Rider Bag Assembly:

Study Group Directions:
Member 1: Color bag.
Member 2: Cut out and fold.
Member 3: Glue sides.
Member 4: Punch holes and string yarn.

Official
Post Rider
Bag

AN OVERVIEW OF COOPERATIVE LEARNING

What makes Cooperative Learning unique?

In a cooperative classroom, group activities are more than just children working together. Learning structures (called recipes here) guide children to respond and interact with each other in specific ways. Every task has both an academic and social goal which are evaluated at the end of the activity with self-monitoring as well as teacher observation.

Instead of competition, students working together learn positive interdependence, that they sink or swim together. Each student contributes his or her part to each activity or assignment. Each team gets a "single grade" based on all the members doing his or her part. Instead of a few top students being the stars, all members must learn and use the information for the group to be successful! Teams even take on the role of instructor, presenting new material or helping teammates practice skills.

The benefits of Cooperative Learning:

In a cooperative classroom, you become a facilitator to learning, not the prime source of instruction. Students begin to see their classmates as important and valuable sources of knowledge. Essential interpersonal social skills learned step-by-step and reinforced in every lesson make the classroom climate become more positive, more nurturing as students learn to give each other encouragement and praise.

Students even benefit academically because in a cooperative atmosphere they have more chances to understand the material through oral rehearsal, thinking out loud, and discussing their views with others in the class. Contact with others' views and ideas increases their tolerance of various learning styles and personal views. Children learn that their differences make for a stronger team.

CLASSROOM GUIDELINES
GROUPING AND SOCIAL SKILLS

Planning for grouping and social skills:

Lessons have been planned for you so that the academic and social skills are "built in" to the activity. This way, even if you have not worked with cooperative learning before, you can organize your groups quickly spending your time monitoring and evaluating social progress.

Team groupings will be suggested for the activities. Primary classrooms work best in pairs because it is easier for children to decide or agree with one other person. Once they are working well in pairs, advance to threes and then 2 sets of pairs to make four. Unless your project needs demand it (such as a culminating activity having five or six distinct parts), four is the suggested upper limit for groups.

When choosing pairs, you may want to choose randomly or assign pairs to mix abilities and temperaments. Occasionally, you will find an "oil and water" pair, or a child who has trouble working with any partner and needs to be changed frequently. Once you have groups of four, make sure they are heterogeneous and have ample opportunity to "gel" as a group and learn to work together. Resist the temptation to break up groups who are having problems. Emphasize the social skills they need to learn and practice to get them all working together.

Defining and developing social skills:

Many teachers shy away from a group approach because they think of all the problems associated with groups of children working together: confusion, noise, personality conflicts, differences of opinion, etc. Cooperative teaching does not assume children have the social skills needed to work together successfully. The behaviors that enhance group progress are introduced, explained, modeled, practiced and evaluated like any other skill.

To use cooperative learning successfully, it will be important for you to be aware of the social skills appropriate for each activity. Introduce them at the beginning of each lesson, define, reinforce and evaluate them at the completion of the assignment. As your groups develop, you may want to emphasize and build on other social skills of your choice. With older groups (grades 4-5), co-op activities are the ideal vehicle to experiment with learning and problem-solving skills. You can introduce these along with the simpler social skills.

These are the Interpersonal Group skills necessary in grades 1-5:

COMING TOGETHER (grades 1-5)
- form groups quietly
- stay in the group
- use quiet voices
- participate
- use names, make eye contact
- speak clearly
- listen actively
- allow no put-downs (encouraging statements)

WORKING TOGETHER (grades 1-5)
- work toward goal, purpose, time limit
- praise others; seek others' ideas
- ask for help when needed
- paraphrase other members' contributions
- energize group
- describe one's feelings when appropriate

LEARNING TOGETHER (grades 3-5)
- summarize material
- seek accuracy by correcting, giving information
- elaborate
- jog memory of teammates
- explain reasons for answer/beliefs
- plan aloud to teach concepts; agree on approaches

PROBLEM-SOLVING SKILLS (grades 4-5)
- criticize ideas, not people
- differentiate where there is disagreement
- integrate a number of ideas into a single conclusion
- ask for justification
- extend another's answer by adding to it.
- probe by asking questions
- generate further answers
- check answers/conclusions with original instruction

Teaching Social Skills:
- Work on one social skill at a time. Add others slowly as groups are ready.
- Introduce the skill and discuss why it is important.
- Define in words and actions what children will see and hear as they are using that skill in their groups. Look through the materials in the classroom management sections to find charts, hand-outs and other materials to help to do this.
- Give a demonstration for the children to follow (modeling).
- Set up practice situations and refer to the charts, etc., as children practice the skill.
- Praise lavishly attempts to use a skill, repeat words/deeds done showing it.
- At the end of the session, give children time to think whether they used the skill in the session or not. Evaluate them by the use of the teacher charts provided or have them "vote" as a group as to whether they think they succeeded and why.
- Be patient with yourself and the students. Social skills need to be practiced often to become natural.

COOPERATIVE GUIDELINES: PREPARING LESSONS

Along with the team grouping suggestions, cooperative recipes for learning (sometimes called practice structures) are used with the activities in this book. The symbol for the recipe is clearly shown on each lesson. The academic and social skill to be emphasized are beside each symbol. This will help you to organize the class and choose the lessons you wish to use.

The recipes provided each reinforce a number of social skills and guide children to process information in their groups in a variety of ways. For the first time through the materials, we suggest you use the recipe with one or two of the social skills listed near the symbol for each activity. However, when you are familiar with the projects, you can emphasize other skills. It is our hope that you will make the lessons your own, adapting them to your particular classroom. As you work through each, they will become natural to you and your students. They will make a positive impact on your classroom atmosphere and student performance. The key is to be patient and give children time to learn and practice each recipe.

COOPERATIVE CLASSROOM RECIPES

Sharing Circle

Social skills: listen actively, participate, clear speech

Group size: Whole class

Directions: Children sit in a large circle, so each student can see the rest. The leader (teacher or student) starts an open-ended statement or sentence, and each student in turn ends it with their own statement. If they can't think of an answer at that time, they can "pass," but are expected to have their answer ready by the time the circle is completed.

Study Group

Social skills: paraphrasing, positive support, time limit, group purpose

Group size: 2-4

Directions: Present information in a traditional way. Children get into their small groups to complete a cooperative assignment which reinforces, expands on or tests their knowledge. Groups can brainstorm, fill out a K W L chart within their groups to set goals for further study or complete various activities like word webbing. Note: use the role cards and discussion strips to help keep social skills moving while in groups. Another quick associations recipe is **Numbered Heads Together.**

Numbered Heads Together

Social Skills: use quiet voices, participate, time limit, quick associations, elaborate, integration, team energizing and praise

Groups: 2-4

Note: For this activity, you will need a code or signal to get all the groups attention: lights on/off, a bell, or hand signal. Use it with other recipes as needed.

Directions: Students are in groups, listening to instruction by teacher. When a question is posed, the teacher tells the groups to put their heads together and discuss it. This gives students a chance to immediately discuss the information and figure out the right response together. After a time is given for discussion, the teacher signals for attention. At this time, students number off within each group. The teacher calls one number, and a representative from each group gives the team's answer. Team points are given for correct responses.

Note: If you want simultaneous responses, have team members write their response on a card and hold it up, or write their solution on the blackboard.

Turn to Your Partner

Social Skills: using names, eye contact, listen actively, quiet voices, paraphrasing

Group size: 2

Directions: As you present material, have students pair up to share ideas, information or opinions. This works best when you use established "partners" who are nearby to keep a minimum of class time to moving toward partners. It is a good way to quickly reinforce active listening and early social skills.

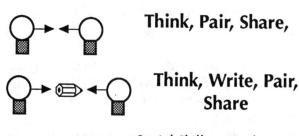

Think, Pair, Share,

Think, Write, Pair, Share

Social Skills: paraphrasing, memory of content, vocalization

Group size: 2

Directions: Similar to "Turn to Your Partner," but when more time is wanted on-task. Present material, have students pair up to think about the content just presented, share ideas, information or opinions. This works well when you use established "partners," but can also be used to exchange pairs to get different opinions. If you have children write down their idea (and it is a good idea, so they won't be swayed, or lose direction), you can "pair" them up with others who think the same thing or have different opinions.

Note: For another way to group by opinion or interest, see **Pick Your Spot**.

Pick Your Spot (Corners)

Social Skills: vocalization, groups by interest or opinion

Group size: 4-6

Note: By having children write down responses ahead of time, they will stay on task better and get to their places quicker. You can see where they're headed and direct them to the right "corner."
Directions: Pose a question or topic with four answers or sub-topics and have each children select which of the four would be their choice. Have them write it down and go the the "corner" of the room where that topic or answer is displayed. This is a quick way to get children of similar interest together to do further study, share opinions or become "roving reporters" to teach the rest of the class.

Note: For another way to group children by interest or opinion see **Line-Ups**.

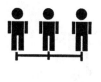

Line-Ups

Social Skills: vocalization, probing for information, sharing reasons for answer

Group size: whole class or spit in half for two "lines"

Note: This works best in probing an answer or problem with a range of opinions.

Directions: Create a masking tape line on your classroom floor divided into three categories; yes/ maybe / no, always / sometimes / never, etc. Pose a question or situation. Have the children write down their answer on small slips of papers. Then have them "line up" on the line that nearest matches their opinion. Once on the line, you can use the information by having them discuss with their immediate group their reasons for choosing that answer, or leave their paper "markers" in place and go back to their desks to look and compare how many are in each section and make a class "opinion graph." Some classroom teachers have developed lively discussions by having the children pair with members from other sections to discuss why they chose differently. The line can remain in place to be used later.

Stand and Share

Social Skills: speak clearly, listen actively, participate, time limit

Group size: 2-4

Directions: As in "Study Group" teams ready themselves on a specific topic. Teams or members within each team number off. When the teacher calls a number, all the team members must stand and be ready to answer the question. As you call the numbers, that team or member answers the questions and sits down. This is good for an oral quiz or checking problems where all members need to know the information.

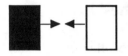

Co-Op Cards

Social Skills: using names, eye contact, positive statements, jog memory

Group size: Do first with partners, then 4.

Note: this format is an invaluable method for memory work and drill; children learn while praising each other and supporting each other's efforts!

Directions: Give each pair or study group a set of the Co-Op Cards you want them to learn. Have them learn to play these games:

Game 1: Maximum Help
Partner 1 hands his card to partner 2. Partner 2, the "teacher," shows the cards and the answers one by one to Partner 1, the "student," who repeats the words or answers. Cards done correctly are "won" back with lots of praise from the "teacher." Cards done incorrectly are repeated and explained thoroughly by the tutor and asked again. When all cards are won back, they switch roles.

Game 2: Minimum Help
Partner 1 hands his card to partner 2. Partner 2, the "teacher," shows the cards one by one to Partner 1, the "student," who answers. Cards done correctly are "won" back with lots of praise from the "teacher." Cards done incorrectly are repeated with some hints. When all cards are won back, they switch roles.

Game 3: No Help
Partner 1 hands his card to partner 2. Partner 2, the "teacher," shows the cards one by one to Partner 1, the "student," who answers. Cards done correctly are "won" back with lots of praise from the "teacher." Cards done incorrectly are put back into the teacher's stack to be repeated with no hints. When all cards are won back, they switch roles.

Evaluation: Groups can keep a chart showing all words learned, with an envelope for those words that still need to be practiced and "won."

Note: To keep the game fresh, the teacher should continually think of new and grander praises!

Pairs Check or Partners

Social Skills: accuracy, energizing, positive support, ways to jog memory

Groups size: 2

Directions: Teams work in pairs. In each pair, one player does a problem. The other is the "coach" in every sense of the word...giving help, praise, and encouragement! Switch roles after every problem. When two problems are completed, pairs must check with each other and agree on the answers. This is a good time to have a team "high sign" or handshake. Then proceed to the next two problems in the same way. Remember to keep your pairs heterogeneous for activities like this...so there is a range of abilities to keep things moving!

Interview

Social Skills: using names, eye contact, paraphrasing, summarizing, describing feelings, probing for answers, vocalization

Group size: 3-4

Note: This format is good for anticipating a unit or to close a unit.

Directions: Members take turns interviewing each other. After they have all had a chance to share, have the group round-robin (described at right) what they learned from the interviews. For example, each child could take on one of the characters from an event or story and give his or her perspective. Use of role cards or discussion strips, so each asks a pertinent question, will help it go smoother.

Round Table

Social Skills: time limit, quick associations, participate, extend another's answers

Group size: 3-4

Directions: All team members contribute ideas to one sheet of paper. Make sure the team members know the directions the paper should be passed. When the signal is given members write or draw the answer and pass it on.

Simultaneous Round Table

Social Skills: time limit, waiting politely, quiet voices, participate

Directions: More than one sheet is passed within the group. Members start with one sheet each, and pass it on.

Round Robin

Social Skills: vocalization, time limit, quick associations, participate, extend another's answers, building team spirit

Group size: 3-4

Directions: This is an oral counterpart to Round Table. Note: this is an excellent method for brainstorming vocabulary, problem solving, or to create an oral story together. It is also excellent for younger students with limited writing skills.

Team Share

Social Skills: planning to teach, elaborate, vocalization, ways to jog memory, extend another's answers, integrate a number of ideas

Group size: 3-4

Note: This is an ideal way to have teams share products or projects with each other. Be sure to give teams time to plan how they will "present" themselves.

Directions: When teams have completed various projects, have them get ready to share it with other teams. Organize the class so each team is clearly marked, and knows where they are to go. For instance, a blue #1 card would goes to one team, a blue #2 card goes to another, and they meet at the "blue" station. Team #1 shares first, team #2 is the "audience." Then they switch. If you have an uneven number of teams, you can pair up with one or put three groups together.

CLASSROOM MANAGEMENT CHARTS AND BUTTONS

These materials will help you define, display, remind and reinforce social lessons. We have themed them to the book for added fun!

Standards T-Chart

How to use: Enlarge and reproduce full-page or poster size. Write the social skill to be learned in the top section as you discuss its importance. Have your classes brainstorm "how it looks" when children are using that skill, as well as "how it sounds" when it's happening. This gives the children a solid basis for modeling and monitoring their social behavior. Display it prominently and refer to it often. Laminate and save. Use the chart whenever that skill is being emphasized.

Social Skills T-Chart

Skill:

LOOKS LIKE: **SOUNDS LIKE:**

PRAISE WORDS

How to Use: In order to increase the kind and frequency of encouraging words in the classroom, brainstorm suggestions and write them in open areas and all around the tree. See the Cavendish Family Tree on page 3. Keep them on display. As you hear others, add them to the chart with plenty of praises of your own!

Talk to others as you would have them talk to you.

Note: For a class with ingrained negative habits, it may also be helpful to put up a list of TABOO or OFF-LIMITS sayings. These can be placed on another chart with a line through them or the title "Cooperative NO-NOs!"

DISCUSSION STRIPS

To Use: Reproduce the strips you will use on as many different colors of paper as there are members of each team. Each student gets appropriate strips to use during groups discussions. Whenever a student contributes, a strip is "spent." Discussion goes on until all have used their strips. This keeps all members contributing equally, as well as having them be aware of *how* they are responding. Note: Younger groups may need practice in many of these modes before it comes naturally to them, so start simply. Have each child bring an envelope from home to store the strips in to be used again.

Answer a Question	*Ask a Question*
Check for Understanding	*Encourage Your Group*
Give a Praiser	*Give an Idea*
Keep Your Group on Task	*Paraphrase*
Respond to an Idea	*Summarize Progress*

EVALUATION TOOLS

TEACHER OBSERVATION FORM

To Use: When your groups are working, use this form to circulate, observe and record their progress. Be sure to write quotes and repeat them to further reinforce and model behavior during and after the activity.

Teacher Observation Chart

Skill: _____

GROUP	STUDENTS	COMMENTS

K-W-L CHART

How to Use: Have the children discuss an upcoming topic and fill in questions for the K, W, and L sections. Reproduce full page size for use in the small groups to focus learning or poster size as a whole-class exercise to introduce a topic.

K= What I KNOW about: _____.
W= WHAT I would like to find out: _____.
L= What I have LEARNED: _____.

ROLE BUTTONS

How to Use: Reproduce on sturdy tagboard and cut out. When children are doing group work, it may help for them to have a visual reminder of their group "job." Use those applicable to the activity and supply them to the groups. You will also find it easier to check if students are performing as they should because you can see at a glance what each member's role is within the group.

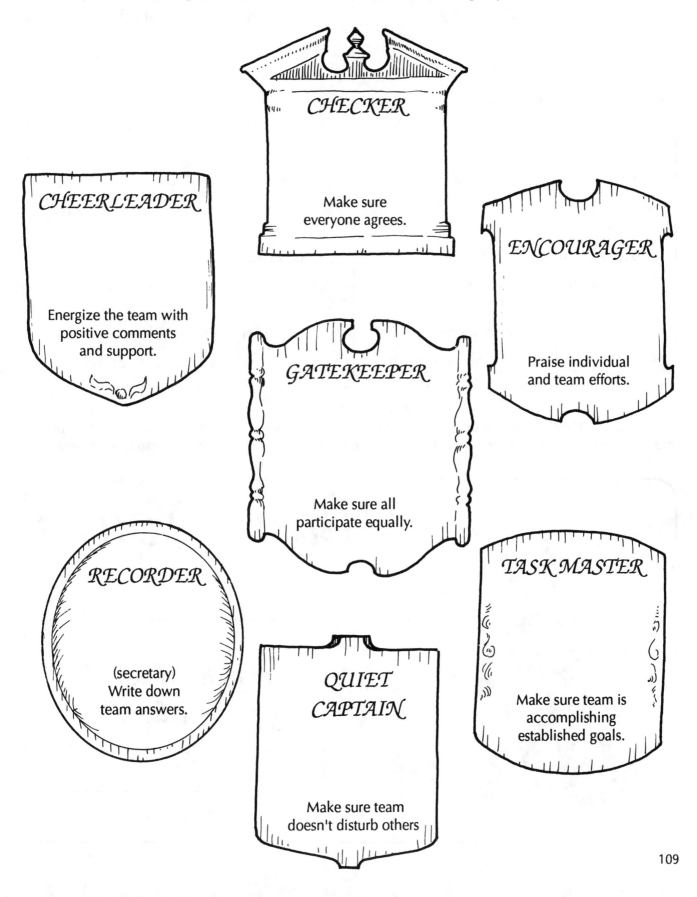

CHECKER

Make sure
everyone agrees.

CHEERLEADER

Energize the team with
positive comments
and support.

ENCOURAGER

Praise individual
and team efforts.

GATEKEEPER

Make sure all
participate equally.

RECORDER

(secretary)
Write down
team answers.

*QUIET
CAPTAIN*

Make sure team
doesn't disturb others

TASK MASTER

Make sure team is
accomplishing
established goals.

GROUP EVALUATION FORM

To Use: Take a few minutes after an activity for teams or individuals to evaluate their progress. The group form should be agreed upon by members, filled in, and initialed by all. The individual from will be helpful when groups are having problems. They'll be able to spot areas needing improvement.

How Are We Doing?	How Am I Doing?
Group: _____ Date: _____	Group: _____ Date: _____
1. We each contributed ideas: often ___ sometimes ___ not very much ___	1. I contributed my ideas: often ___ sometimes ___ not very much ___
2. We listened to each other: often ___ sometimes ___ not very much ___	2. I listened to my partners: often ___ sometimes ___ not very much ___
3. We encouraged each other: often ___ sometimes ___ not very much ___	3. I encouraged my partners: often ___ sometimes ___ not very much ___
4. We built on each other's ideas: often ___ sometimes ___ not very much ___	4. I built on my partners' ideas: often ___ sometimes ___ not very much ___

AWARD CERTIFICATE

How to Use: When you see groups working and accomplishing goals, give them a visual reminder of their progress. Groups can earn them, barter them, display them with team pride or use toward whole-class goals.

Thank You,

_____

*for making this class
a friendly place to learn!*

signed _____

date _____

Selected Bibliography

Many reference materials were used in the preparation of this book. You may find the following titles appropriate for your students. Your librarian will be able to help you select others.

American Popular Music: The Beginning Years, Berenice Robinson Morris, New York, Franklin Watts, Inc., 1962.

Colonial Craftsmen, and the Beginnings of American Industry, Edwin Tunis, New York, World Publishing Company, 1965.

Colonial Living, Edwin Tunis, New York, Thomas Y. Crowell Company, 1957.

Early American Crafts, Tools, Shops and Products, C. B. Colby, New York, Coward-McCann, Inc., 1967.

Home and Child Life in Colonial Days, Shirley Glubok, New York, The Macmillan Company, 1969.

Hot Cross Buns and Other Old Street Cries, John Langstaff, New York, Atheneum, 1978.

If You Lived in Colonial Times, Ann McGovern, New York, The Four Winds Press, 1971.

Life in Colonial America, Elizabeth George Speare, New York, Random House, 1963.

The Black Man in America 1619-1790, Florence and J. B. Jackson, New York, Franklin Watts, Inc., 1970.

The Golden Book of Colonial Crafts, Family Creative Workshop, New York Western Publishing Company, Inc.,1975.

The Tavern and the Ferry, Edwin Tunis, New York, Thomas Y. Crowell Company, 1973.

Young Paul Revere's Boston, Sam and Beryl Epstein, Champaign, Illinois, Garrard Publishing Company, 1966.

Cooperative Learning References

Circles of Learning, Cooperation in the Classroom, David W. Johnson, Roger T. Johnson, Edythe Johnson Holubec, Patricia Roy, Alexandria, Virginia, Association for Supervision and Curriculum Development, 1984.

Cooperative Learning: Getting Started, Susan Ellis and Susan Whalen, New York, Scholastic Inc., 1990.

Cooperative Learning Lessons for Little Ones, Lorna Curan, San Juan Capistrano, California, Resources for Teachers, 1990.

Cooperative Learning Resources for Teachers, Spencer Kagan, PhD., San Juan Capistrano, California, 1989.

INDEX